Taking
Control of
Your Time

The Results-Driven Manager Series

The Results-Driven Manager series collects timely articles from *Harvard Management Update* and *Harvard Management Communication Letter* to help senior to middle managers sharpen their skills, increase their effectiveness, and gain a competitive edge. Presented in a concise, accessible format to save managers valuable time, these books offer authoritative insights and techniques for improving job performance and achieving immediate results.

Other books in the series:

Teams That Click

Presentations That Persuade and Motivate

Face-to-Face Communications for Clarity and Impact

Winning Negotiations That Preserve Relationships

Managing Yourself for the Career You Want

Getting People on Board

Dealing with Difficult People

A Timesaving Guide

THE RESULTS-DRIVEN MANAGER

Taking
Control of
Your Time

Harvard Business School Press

Boston, Massachusetts

Library of Congress Cataloging-in-Publication Data

The results-driven manager: taking control of your time.
    p.   cm. — (The results-driven manager series)
    ISBN 1-59139-635-2 (alk. paper)
    1. Time management. I. Title: Taking control of your time.
  II. Series.
  HD69.T54R47 2005
  658.4'093—dc22

                        2004013696

Contents

Contents

Tackling Specific Time-Management Challenges

Making Smarter Decisions Faster

Preventing Burnout

Taking
Control of
Your Time

Introduction

۞   ۞   ۞

Imagine someone asking you what you consider the most frustrating aspect of your job. Would you respond with something like, "I just don't have enough time in my workday to take care of all my responsibilities"? If so, you're not alone. In today's rapidly shifting business landscape, more and more managers are feeling that they've lost control of their time. In fact, the problem seems to be taking on epidemic proportions.

What does loss of control over your time look like in practical terms? Perhaps you're finding yourself sitting in ever more meetings that turn out to be unproductive, unnecessary, and way too long. Or you can't seem to respond to all those cell-phone, voice mail, and e-mail messages that stack up the minute you turn your back. Maybe you're having difficulty setting direction for your team or making decisions. Or you can't find that one vital document your boss asked for amid the piles of paperwork and clutter on your desk. And what about the mounds of trade journals, newspapers, reports, and other materials you're supposed to read if you have any hope of staying current with industry trends?

The High Cost of Runaway Time

If these scenarios describe your work life, then you *and* your company are likely paying a high price. The stress that comes with feeling that you've lost control of your time can lead to physical and mental health problems, which, if ignored, often set the stage for burnout. Equally troubling, your entire organization loses money. Consider the cost of time-wasting meetings: One firm calculated that a work group was racking up $390 each time it convened. That amounted to $20,000 per year, given that the group consisted of five members averaging $70,000 a year in salary and that their meetings lasted two hours.

But personal stress and companywide financial losses aren't the only costs. Losing control of your time can take its toll on your direct reports as well. Specifically, you have more difficulty analyzing information, making smart decisions, and defining a clear direction for your team. Distracted by immediate demands on your already scarce time, you neglect your *real* responsibilities: identifying ways in which your team can help support the company's big-picture concerns, strategic aims, and long-term objectives. Planning, thinking, and decision making are all driven to the micro level—focusing your attention on details rather than higher-level concerns and your team's needs.

Controlling Your Time, Gaining Results

Contrast the dire scenarios just mentioned with the results you generate for your company when you win back control of your time: You provide a clear sense of direction and make smart decisions quickly. You stay focused on strategic, long-term concerns, rather than getting pulled into short-term, micro-level details. You find yourself better able to anticipate what will next be required of you—and thus strengthen your ability to formulate more effective plans for your department and team. And you experience far less stress and irritability—staving off health problems and burnout.

Everyone wins. *You* do, because you experience much more enjoyment in your job. Your *direct reports* benefit, because you have more time and energy to devote to helping them develop their skills and work together effectively as a team. And your *company* wins, because you can now stay focused on the activities required to align your department and team behind the corporate strategy.

So how can you take the first steps toward regaining control of your time—and reaping the benefits for yourself and your firm? One way is to implement fundamental time-management strategies—such as breaking your job responsibilities into distinct categories (e.g., managing people, taking care of administrative tasks) and deciding what percentage of your time you should be spending in each category. Additional time-management strategies include creating professional mission statements and checking your activities against them every week.

But fundamental strategies aren't enough on their own. You also need to adapt your tactics to the specific time-management challenge in question. For instance, making meetings productive requires very different approaches than coping with message overload or figuring out how to deal with all that reading you've fallen behind on.

You can also work to "win back" some of that lost time by learning how to make smarter decisions faster—for example, by using communications technology to merge your managerial knowledge with that of other managers and encourage information sharing. Finally, you can establish disciplines that help you manage the stress that comes with time pressure—and thereby take active steps to prevent burnout.

The four sections of this collection contain articles that help you with each of these areas—applying fundamental time-management strategies, adapting your time-management tactics to specific challenges, making smarter decisions faster, and keeping burnout at bay. Here's a roadmap to guide you through the articles.

Fundamental Strategies for Managing Your Time

Experts have developed a wealth of potent strategies for managing time, and the articles in the first section of this book are brimming with recommendations. MIT Sloan School lecturer Melissa Raffoni starts things off with tried-and-true tips in "Be Sure You're Spending Your Time in the Right Places." Raffoni outlines a three-step plan for allocating your time: 1) Break your job responsibilities into categories such as "growth and improvement," "managing people," "daily responsibilities," and "administration." 2) Ask yourself what percentage of your time should be spent in each category—and be willing to change these allocations weekly, monthly, or quarterly if conditions warrant it. 3) Check for alignment with your superiors and colleagues by getting their input on your allocations. Then do what it takes to execute your plan—such as learning to say "No" to colleagues who are given to making impromptu requests for your time.

In "Strategies for the Shorthanded," editor Paul Michelman describes additional time-management tactics, including a five-part litmus test for prioritizing your goals developed by manager Cheryl Andrus. To determine which of your many goals are truly critical—to you, your team, and your company—ask: "What is the goal's economic impact?" "Is the goal aligned with the company's strategy?" "How will this goal satisfy stakeholders?" "How much passion, talent, and energy do I have for this goal?" and "Do we have the resources to achieve the goal?"

Jim Billington's "Timeless Insights on How to Manage Your Time" provides additional weapons for your time-management arsenal. For example, before launching any important piece of work, visualize the desired end result. Then ask how each of your undertakings fits into that envisioned outcome. Consult others as you do your imagining—to ensure that everyone has the same outcome in mind.

In "Getting Organized," Constantine von Hoffman shares recommendations for keeping your workspace clutter-free. By organizing your physical workspace, you enhance your ability to quickly find a particular piece of information your boss needs, as well as to collaborate more efficiently with others on a project. Suggestions include resisting the urge to use your desk as a file-storage area and periodically purging your files of documents and information that are no longer useful or pertinent to your work.

Tackling Specific
Time-Management Challenges

In the second section of the book, you'll discover ways to deal with particular kinds of time-management challenges. In "How to Make Every Meeting Matter," Swarthmore College news and information director Tom Krattenmaker presents tips for getting the most value out of all those meetings. Most meetings, Krattenmaker maintains, "are inefficient, unfocused time drains. . . . Yet at their best, meetings can mean everything to an organization."

How to make sure that the meetings *you* lead or attend enhance—rather than hinder—your firm's success? For one thing, before you call a meeting, ask whether the purpose of the meeting could be fulfilled some other way—such as through e-mail, memos, or informal conversations. If so, don't call the meeting. Also, insist that meeting participants do more than just discuss the topic at hand. In Krattenmaker's words, "Define clear objectives toward which people can work and against which they can measure progress," and end with agreed-upon action. To control "meetings creep," some firms are also experimenting with declaring meeting-free days or designating certain hours of the day as off-limits for meetings.

Meetings aren't the only "time sink" by any means. In "Managing Message Overload," industrial psychologist Dwight Moore addresses the question of how to handle the flood of messages that new communication technologies—especially e-mail—have made possible. As Moore explains, "Most communications in today's electronic world are one-way rather than interactive. . . . Since the sender generally expects a response, [these messages] create a sense of urgency. We leap to answer our messages before we do anything else."

To regain control, Moore advises, begin your day differently—by defining a strategic goal and developing a plan for achieving it, instead of jumping to your e-mail. Handle e-mails at the end of the day, not the beginning. And teach people how to send you e-mails. For instance, one executive codes his responses "1" for "Keep sending me this kind of information"; "2" for "Unless I'm on this team, don't send me such information"; "3" for "Send this to the responsible person on my staff"; and so on.

Like "message overload," "infoglut"—or the tidal wave of information generated by the Internet and other online or print publishing advances—can make you further lose your grip on time. Indeed, as Edward Prewitt writes in "Coping with Infoglut: Learn from the Folks in Financial Services," "Information overload impairs the brain's ability to perform tasks like analysis and decision making."

Prewitt offers eight tips for fighting back. For instance, narrow your list of daily information sources down to the crucial few that contain the data most critical to your job. In addition, challenge the assumption that printed or online information is the best way to keep your business knowledge up-to-date. "Two-way conversations with . . . people," Prewitt argues, "will generally be superior." People are interactive. Articles aren't. "There's no substitute for face-to-face." Prewitt also recommends using online "push sites" to profile your specific information needs. These sites allow Web operators to send you only the news and data that fit your outline.

In addition to meetings, message overload, and infoglut, a phenomenon we might call "task overload" can also present distinct time-management challenges. In "Is Multitasking Overrated?" business writer Jennifer McFarland maintains that trying to deal with multiple tasks by jumping back and forth among them only hampers your productivity. "Even a 30-second distraction," she writes, "can be enough to derail you . . . . Like a boiling pot of water, your brain needs time to warm up again afterward. . . . The associated costs can add up to as much as two to four hours a day." McFarland offers suggestions for battling task overload, such as delegating everything you don't need to do personally and blocking off periods of time when you won't get interrupted.

Making Smarter Decisions Faster

By augmenting fundamental and situation-specific time-management strategies with tactics for making smarter decisions faster, you can reclaim some of that lost time—and put it to potent use. The articles in the third section of this collection focus on speeding up the decision-making process—without giving up decision-making *skill*.

Edward Prewitt starts the section with his article "Fast-Cycle Decision Making," in which he explains how to make good choices even as your business changes quickly. Prewitt presents insights from leading management thinkers and practitioners on how to "act wisely, even in the face of insufficient time and inadequate data."

For example, Percy Barnevik, CEO of Asea Brown Boveri, advocates changing the way you think about speedy decisions. "It's better to make a decision quickly and be right seven times out of ten than to delay while searching for the perfect solution," he tells *his* managers. "A decision delayed is a decision forgone." Some companies are also handing decision-making power over to potential customers, further stepping up the pace of the decision process. To illustrate, "Putting a prototype in the market and getting a reaction and letting the market shape it, even to the point of identifying the bugs and in some cases suggesting fixes . . . accelerates your decision making so you're responding to market information first rather than at the end of the decision cycle."

In "Speed Leading: Do You Have What It Takes?" Accenture senior research fellow Robert J. Thomas and University of Southern California professor Warren Bennis present additional guidelines for fast direction setting and decision making. According to the authors, "speed leaders" confront messy or unfamiliar decision situations with an approach that Thomas and Bennis call "ALA"—for act, learn, and adapt. Through ALA, you "experiment in order to advance knowledge, . . . constantly being on the lookout for 'things you don't know you don't know.'"

You can also accelerate decision making by learning from a variety of sources. How? Practice seeing the world from many different perspectives—your own; those of your subordinates and peers; and those of your customers and other individuals. Constantly putting yourself in others' shoes "creates a tension—an edginess" that drives you to look for previously unseen conditions.

Perhaps no situation demands fast but smart decision making more than when you've just started a challenging new job at a struggling company. In "Advice to Leaders in New Jobs: Act Fast When the Economy Is Slow," Jennifer McFarland provides strategies for "hitting the ground running" in your new role. As she explains, it's vital to "have people energized and focused on solving important business problems within your first six months."

How to implement a "fast-break philosophy without steamrolling the people you need most"? Learn as much as you can about the strategic issues facing your unit or organization *before* your first day on the job. Negotiate this transitional time with your new employer, and use it to talk with people throughout the organization, as well as with individuals who have left it. But resist any urge to assume that you have to arrive with all the answers. Believing that you can "do it all on your own" can lead to your downfall. Instead, "come prepared with a sense of what needs to be done, but allow for the fact that you still have learning to do"—which you can do by making room for others' advice.

In "Don't Throw Good Money (or Time) After Bad," Jimmy Guterman provides additional recommendations for making savvy decisions under pressure. In particular, managers tend to make unwise decisions after significant amounts of money or time have been invested in an effort that has soured. How to avoid this "sunk-cost" trap—so that you don't escalate your firm's commitment to a product, person, or strategy beyond a reasonable point? Resist any urge to make decisions merely to justify past decisions. And watch for a tendency to equate time with money—you become more susceptible to the sunk-cost trap when you make this association.

In the final article in this section—"Which Projects Get Top Billing?"—editor Paul Michelman addresses the unique challenges of deciding which projects should go at the top of your priority list. He outlines a process for making this crucial decision, which includes steps such as considering how each potential project aligns behind your company's corporate strategy, choosing projects that will exert the most immediate impact, and jointly prioritizing projects with your boss.

Preventing Burnout

None of the strategies you'll learn about in the first three sections of this book can provide full value if you don't also take steps to manage the stress that comes with time pressure—stress that can lead to burnout. You can't eliminate *all* stress from your job, nor would you want to. (A certain degree of stress can actually be useful.) The articles in the fourth section of this collection set forth daily mental disciplines and routines that can help you keep stress from reaching destructive levels.

In the first article of this section, "Making Sense of Your Time Bind, and Escaping It," David Stauffer recommends attitude changes and practices that can further help take the edge off time-related stress. To illustrate, he advises "reversing your relationship to time." In his words, "Move away from the idea that certain activities must continually give way to the 'demands' of other activities. Move toward the idea that activities you value are as important as what you feel compelled to do; indeed, that they are inviolable."

To shift your thinking as Stauffer describes, "change your self-talk" by employing "affirmations"—positive statements, such as "I'm in control of how I spend my time," that you repeat to yourself. In addition, acknowledge that you can't "do it all"—and remind yourself assertively that that's okay. The alternative? "Narrow your field" by making tough choices about what most merits your attention. You can also practice resisting "the progressive need for task completion"—or "hurry sickness"—by learning to enjoy the doing, not just the getting done. Problems and delays are part of life; when you come to terms with that fact, you experience significantly less stress.

Stauffer adds to his recommendations with "Pump Up Your Volume! A Dozen Ideas for Boosting Personal Productivity." In this article, you'll find a wealth of tips for keeping time-related stress under control. Examples include practicing preventive "medicine" by establishing—and sticking to—good health habits, such as exercising regularly and eating responsibly. Stauffer also advises matching your best times of the day (when you feel most energized and focused) to your most demanding work, while relegating your worst times of the day to "mindless work."

Additional tips in this article include refreshing yourself with "fun and child-like play," along with connecting with others to ease unproductive worrying. As Harvard Medical School lecturer Edward M. Hallowell told Stauffer while being interviewed for this article, "Connectedness . . . a feeling of being part of something larger than yourself" can neutralize the negative effects of worry. How to cultivate connectedness? Say hello to colleagues in the workplace. Set up lunch dates. Ask for advice. According to Hallowell, "Without connectedness, you worry. With it, you thrive."

In the final article in this section, "Five Questions About Encouraging Managers to Delegate with Jeffrey Pfeffer," the Stanford University organizational behavior professor shares his insights on another source of time pressure that can heighten stress and ultimately cause burnout: managerial failure to delegate. Many managers, Pfeffer says, "have a natural reluctance to delegate responsibility," because their organization venerates "heroic leaders." Managers who have been given visible perks such as elegant offices and reserved parking frequently find it difficult to "entrust responsibility to subordinates whose trappings are significantly inferior to their own." The consequence? Managers take on more and more of their direct reports' problems and responsibilities—and subject themselves to increasing time pressure.

To combat these forces, start by examining your own attitudes toward delegation. Challenge any assumptions you may be harboring about how your company will view you if you begin delegating more. The fact is, delegating is good for you, your direct reports, *and* your company. As Pfeffer explains, "Giving people more responsibility for making decisions in their jobs generates greater productivity, morale, and commitment." Your company can also take steps to cultivate an environment that invites delegation. For example, assigning managers larger staffs and more responsibility makes it harder for them to micromanage. And eliminating status symbols sends the message that the firm has an egalitarian culture, which encourages delegating.

Clearly, taking control of your time isn't easy. Numerous forces—including the accelerating pace of business, cultural expectations and attitudes, and technological advances—have conspired to make it harder than ever for managers to control their time, rather than *being* controlled by it. Yet the problem *is* surmountable—if you establish and practice time-management disciplines and take a cold-eyed look at your own attitudes toward time.

And just as you can learn to prioritize your on-the-job responsibilities, you can prioritize how you'll attack your thorniest time-management problems. For example, if the many suggestions in this collection's articles seem overwhelming, start by selecting several powerful tactics related to the specific time-management problem that you consider your worst—such as unproductive meetings, message overload, or infoglut. If stress is your most pressing time-related problem, focus your energies on preventing burnout. And if you're in a situation where speedy, smart decision making is particularly crucial, concentrate on learning to make the wisest choices given the limited time or inadequate information at hand.

After you've read the articles in this collection, take a moment to think about how you'll begin applying the strategies you've discovered. Ask yourself, "What are my most difficult time-management problems? What are these problems costing my company in terms of financial losses, decreased productivity, or sagging morale? Which techniques would provide the *most* leverage for my particular situation? What changes can I make now to regain control of my time?"

As with any managerial skill, learning to take control of your time requires practice. It also takes tolerance for a bit of trial and error—a willingness to pick and choose among the many different techniques, to see which ones work best for you. But as many formerly time-strapped managers have discovered, the effort yields valuable benefits—for you, your team, *and* your organization.

Fundamental Strategies for Managing Your Time

To help beleaguered managers, time-management experts have developed a veritable arsenal of techniques and tools for regaining control of your time. No matter which time-management challenges are most pressing for you, the strategies described in this section's articles can help.

In particular, you'll find a wealth of recommendations for prioritizing the many goals that you're trying to achieve as part of your managerial responsibilities. Prioritizing—including deciding which efforts are most important to your company's strategic objectives—enables you to allocate your time proactively rather than merely react to pressures as they come along. Another theme that emerges from this section centers on the importance of keeping your workspace organized—which translates directly into saved time.

Be Sure You're Spending Your Time in the Right Places

○   ○   ○

Melissa Raffoni

"Client acquisition used to take up 20% of my time," says Allan Huntley, CEO of Abacus Travel in Peabody, Massachusetts. "But because of the downturn, our client volume has shrunk by more than 25%. As a result, I've become very focused on managing the top line. Client acquisition now takes up 40% to 50% of my time."

With regional economies throughout the world experiencing the doldrums, more than a few executives are beating the bushes in an attempt to replace lost revenue. But Huntley is also speaking to a larger challenge: the need to be able to keep your time allocation in tune with current conditions. The prolonged market correction can certainly be disheartening, but it can also serve as a clarion call to managers to implement a corresponding correction in where they're placing most of their effort.

Although most managers understand intellectually that time is their scarcest resource, few make the effort to get on the balcony to gain a strategic perspective on how they spend their hours each week. And still fewer make a regular practice of holding the mirror up to their faces, that is, keeping track of how the priorities they say are most important jibe with the way they actually spend their time.

"Those we label natural born leaders know how to leverage their time," writes Warren Blank in *The 108 Skills of Natural Born Leaders*. For those in whom this talent is not innate, here's how to craft a plan for leveraging your time.

1: Break your job responsibilities into distinct categories.

The categories will vary depending on your job function, but they must be both strategic and tactical—identify no more than six.

Growth and Improvement

This category focuses on opportunities, not on crises, and it's often the one in which the added value you bring to your unit or company is the greatest. For a product manager, it's the time spent innovating; for an operations manager, it's the time spent improving processes; for the senior executive, it's the time spent on strategy. The challenge is to keep the time allotted to these high-leverage activities sacrosanct—don't let more pressing, but less important, needs crowd them out.

> To-do lists will be only marginally useful unless you time-box them. Set parameters for how much time you plan to devote to each task.

Managing People

You may want to break down this category into three smaller ones: managing up, managing across, and managing down. Managers are well aware that coaching and mentoring enable them to maximize their leverage, but especially in times of belt tightening it helps to be reminded that you can't create efficiencies without upward and lateral alignment. Moreover, everyone agrees that communication is critical, but how many people actually plan time for it? In your haste to make your numbers, don't let your communication—in any of these three directions—falter.

Primary Day-to-Day Responsibilities

Depending on your role, this area could also be subdivided—say, into selling *and* delivering services.

Administration

This includes necessary chores such as assessing your department's resource needs, interviewing job candidates, responding to letters and e-mail, filling out time sheets and expense reports, and writing performance evaluations. Get ready for a shock when you add up all the hours.

2: Ask yourself what percentage of your time you should be spending in each category.

Before you assign percentages, ask yourself this question, recommends Blank: "Given what I truly want to accomplish today as a leader, what will be the best use of my time?" To answer it, factor in the competing claims on your time: the activities that enable you to generate the most leverage, the company's strategic priorities, and the short-term needs of your supervisors, direct reports, and customers. Once you've assigned percentages, translate them into hourly figures for each category. Is the total number of hours realistic and sustainable for the time frame you're considering?

To be useful, your time allocations may need to change quarterly, monthly, or even weekly. "Early this year, our sales team experienced difficulty in closing new clients," says Huntley. "As a result, I got much more involved. Now, I spend an entire day every week in sales and marketing meetings."

3: Check for alignment with your superiors and colleagues.

Run your time allocations by your manager and key colleagues; ask them to share theirs, if possible. Sharing time allocations with members of his leadership team gives the group focus and cohesion, says Huntley. "I get progress reports from short weekly meetings of the executive team. Based on those updates, I allocate how to spend my time for the next week or so."

Now that you have a plan for leveraging your time, all you need to do is be ruthless in your execution of it.

Audit Your Time

Take out last week's calendar and evaluate it using your newly established time allocations for each category. This will give you a sense of how much adjustment will be necessary going forward, record how you spend your time in a time-management log—for many, this very discipline is half the battle (*see* Sample Weekly Time Log for a Management Consultant). "The last time I kept a time log, I was surprised to learn that when I am in the office I spend almost half of my time on the telephone, either taking calls or leaving messages for people who aren't available," writes Elaine Biech in *The Consultant's Quick Start Guide.*

Time audits, adds Blank, can also "reveal when and how you get distracted from things that matter." For instance, is multitasking really helping you manage better? This skill is regularly held up as the *sine qua non* of modern-day managerial aptitudes, but a study by Joshua Rubinstein, David Meyer, and Jeffrey Evans indicates that people experience something akin to writer's block whenever they have to switch from one task to another. The more complicated the task you're switching from or to, the greater the time cost, that is, the longer it takes you shift over to the new task, adopt its mindset, and then get warmed up again once you return to the original task. All told, the study estimates, these switching costs could reduce a company's efficiency by 20% to 40%.

Sample Weekly Time Log for a Management Consultant

Category	Time allocation percentage / hours per week	Actual time spent hours							Total percentage / hours per week
		M	Tu	W	Th	F	S	S	
Growth and improvement project methodology, project management	10% / 4 hours		1						2.5% / 1
People (down-team)	5% / 2 hours	0.5	1			0.5			5% / 2
People (up and across)	5% / 2 hours	0.5		1		0.5			5% / 2
Sales support	15% / 6 hours	1	2	2		1			15% / 6
Consulting delivery and client management	60% / 24 hours	3	4	5	7	4			57.5% / 23
Administration	5% / 2 hours	3			1	1	1		15% / 6
Total	100% / 40 hours	8	8	8	8	7	1		100% / 40

Where does the time go? For this consultant, administrative tasks are cutting into the time available for growth and improvement.

Practice Time-Boxing

To-do lists will be only marginally useful if you don't set parameters for how much time to devote to each task. When you make your list, carefully estimate the time each task will take and box it into your calendar. This discipline will not only help you to finish your list, but it will improve your ability to estimate time and manage expectations of those around you. Particularly if you are in a new position or are confronting new tasks, ask for help estimating the time for each task—otherwise, you run the risk of missing deadlines, and mismanaging expectations, badly.

Pay Attention to the Areas Where You're Weakest

If you always delegate the tasks you don't do well, your weak points will haunt you throughout your career. Acknowledge your weaknesses, but use structure to shore them up. For example, many managers have difficulty saying no to colleagues who are skilled at making impromptu requests for time. Let these people know what your priorities for leveraging your time are, and encourage them to schedule meetings with you in advance.

"Most people manage their lives by crises," writes Stephen Covey in *Principle Centered Leadership*. "The only priority setting they do is between one problem and another." But effective managers focus on opportunities, he adds, and they structure their schedules accordingly.

"Unless something more important—not something more urgent—comes along, we must discipline ourselves to do as we planned."

For Further Reading

The Consultant's Quick Start Guide: An Action Plan for Your First Year in Business by Elaine Biech (2001, Jossey-Bass/ Pfeiffer)

The 108 Skills of Natural Born Leaders by Warren Blank (2001, AMACOM)

Principle Centered Leadership by Stephen R. Covey (1991, Summit Books)

"Executive Control of Cognitive Processes in Task Switching" by Joshua S. Rubinstein, David E. Meyer, and Jeffrey E. Evans (*Journal of Experimental Psychology: Human Perception and Performance* Vol. 27, No. 4, August 2001)

Reprint U0110D

Strategies for the Shorthanded

○   ○   ○

Paul Michelman

Meet Cheryl Andrus: Manager. Survivor. A vice president responsible for corporate and product marketing at FranklinCovey, Andrus was asked in August 2002 to also take charge of one of the company's business lines. Along with these new responsibilities came the mandate to achieve 50% bottom-line improvement during the next year.

To do this, Andrus knew she would need a focused and dedicated team. What she had was an overburdened one. In fact, a company survey showed that 60% of Andrus's 48 reports believed that they were working at maximum capacity and couldn't take on any additional work. (The nationwide average in FranklinCovey's xQ survey was 50%.)

What's more, over the course of the next six months, the size of Andrus's already overtaxed staff would shrink from 48 to 35—but corporate expectations would not be ratcheted down.

Andrus had quite a challenge on her hands. Perhaps you are attempting to manage your way through a similarly exigent scenario. Trying to accomplish everything that used to be done by two or three people, you may be feeling stressed, maybe more than a bit underappreciated. But take heart: You can weather this storm and come out on top—if you have a strategy.

A well thought out plan for managing yourself, your team, and even your boss through these tough times will not only help you address the new demands being heaped upon you, it will also help you turn this onerous situation into a springboard for future growth.

Let's begin with what you shouldn't do: "The sure recipe for failure is to suck it up and try to do it all," says Isabel Parlett of Parlance Training, a firm specializing in business communications. "You'll burn out, your team will resent you, your reputation will suffer, and the work probably won't all get done anyway."

Conversely, if you offer resistance to new duties when the company is down, you may not like the company's reaction. Even if you don't find yourself on the wrong end of a future workforce reduction, you'll likely be tagged with the dreaded "not a team player" label, and future opportunities could be severely limited.

So what's the recipe for successful self-management in this economic climate? The ingredients include balance, focus, effective communication, and more than a pinch of dynamism.

Those were certainly apparent in Andrus's response to her rather large dilemma. "I had a problem," she says, "but there were very specific things I focused on to help me through the dark days and deliver value to the company." Here are two facets of her approach.

1: Stay Focused

Since Andrus clearly could not accomplish everything on her agenda, she says she brought "very intense" focus to determining which of her many goals were truly critical— to her, her team, and the company. To do so, she applied a five-part litmus test to each of her existing goals by asking these questions:

- "WHAT IS ITS ECONOMIC IMPACT?" How will this goal affect the company economically and move it forward?

- "IS IT ALIGNED WITH THE COMPANY'S STRATEGY?" In a time of rapidly shifting corporate strategy, it's essential to regularly reevaluate individual and team goals to ensure that each still maps to those of the company.

○ "HOW WILL IT SATISFY STAKEHOLDERS?" How important is it to your boss, your team, and other interested parties?

○ "WHAT IS MY LEVEL OF PASSION, TALENT, AND ENERGY FOR IT?" If you can't bring all three to the table, you're not going to achieve a high return on your efforts.

○ "DO WE HAVE THE RESOURCES?" Is there sufficient time, money, and any other necessary resources to accomplish this goal?

Ultimately, you can't determine which goals rate as must-do's entirely on your own, Andrus says. "After I go through this process myself, I go see my boss to make sure I'm aligned with him and with his stakeholders. You have to learn to be open and to listen to how your boss reacts to your analysis. By focusing on economic impact and strategy in particular, you are talking in his language, and it makes you look smart."

Many managers are daunted by the prospect of having these types of conversations with their bosses, notes Thomas DeLong, who teaches organizational behavior at Harvard Business School. "I'm amazed that although organizations are willing to set metrics for success in difficult times, so few individuals are willing to have conversations about what they need to accomplish," he says.

The toughest thing for most people is initiating this type of discussion, DeLong continues. In his work with professional service firms, he's found that many people would rather work 80 hours per week than hold difficult conversations about their workload.

So how do you broach this delicate subject? "When in doubt, share the dilemma," DeLong says.

For example, you might start a conversation with your boss like this: "I'm excited about the opportunities I have. But I have 10 great opportunities and the time for four. If you were me, how would you approach this?"

2: Remember the Little Picture

At a time when her team was filled with fear and feeling burnt out, Andrus used small successes as a motivational tool. First, make sure everyone understands the long-term strategy, she says. Then, "if you get people focused on current results, even small milestones and successes can get people energized really quickly."

Andrus practices what her company's products preach: She holds both regular team meetings and one-on-ones with her direct reports; she also underscores the importance of having daily and weekly priorities. It's all part of making sure that short-term objectives support long-term goals.

Andrus's strategy appears to be working well. She still has her sanity, and her team is moving ahead: "It's been a slow start, but we're making faster progress every month. So far it looks like we can make it [to the 50% improvement] by the end of the year."

Best Practices

Andrus's experiences and the strategy she employed dovetail nicely with the best advice we heard from a number of self-management experts. Here are their suggestions for overburdened managers.

Get Out in Front

"No one in the organization wants to be the one to decide what has to give" when there is a loss of staff, says Parlance Training's Parlett. "So everyone plays corporate hot potato, passing the problem down the line until someone ends up as the scapegoat for not pulling off a miracle. Stepping up to the plate and making the call about what gets done and what doesn't can make you the hero. You do the deed no one else wants to do, and you focus your efforts toward producing the results you've decided are most meaningful."

Create Alliances

"Senior managers should develop networks of internal alliances," says Larraine Segil, author of *Dynamic Leader, Adaptive Organization: Ten Essential Traits for Managers* (John Wiley, 2002). These are cross-group relationships that are strategically mapped to include stakeholders with direct relationships to managers' areas of influence. Such internal alliances not only augment your current efforts, they also help your work get noticed.

"Keeping your head down under the burden of responsibilities will mean that your personal and strategic vision will be stymied within your own organization," Segil notes. If you miss the opportunity to court key opinion influencers, they won't be able to assist you when you need help later.

DeLong urges executives to create support networks of "truth speakers." Within your organization, you should seek out two or three people "who will tell you the things you don't want to hear and who will give a fair representation of who you are when you're not in the room," he says. "The last thing we need when things are tough is to have people tell us what they think we want to hear."

Manage Up

"Remind your superiors about your added responsibilities," says Susan Battley, CEO of Battley Performance

Consulting, and a leadership psychologist for many *Fortune* 100 firms. "Human nature being what it is, they are likely to forget or overlook this change if you don't." This can be tricky since you don't want to be seen as a whiny opportunist during difficult times. Seek regular feedback from your boss about your expanded duties, Battley recommends. "This can be a subtle and effective reminder," she says; it keeps your new duties in the forefront of your superior's often frazzled mind while ensuring that you are contributing in the most effective way possible.

> Regular team meetings, along with plenty of one-on-ones, help ensure that short-term objectives support long-term goals.

Focus on Your New Duties

The easiest thing to do when you're saddled with new projects is to give them short shrift. In the name of survival, it is tempting to make sure you know enough to manage current processes and leave it at that. This approach misses a big opportunity, says Felicia Zimmerman, author of *Reinvent Your Work: How to Rejuvenate, Revamp, or Recreate Your Career* (Dearborn Trade Publishing, 2001) and principal of Zimmerman Communication.

If you take the time to really understand your team's responsibilities, you can bring a fresh perspective on how to make their work more strategically valuable. "Get the team focused on what they could do differently to provide better results with greater efficiency," says Zimmerman. By doing this, you deliver more value today and set yourself up to deliver more value tomorrow.

To Position Yourself, Begin with Your Team

When you are taking on substantial new responsibilities, it's tempting to fancy yourself an essential component of the company's survival—or at least its short-term success. However, Zimmerman cautions against attempting to take advantage of this situation until you have shown concrete results. And when you do make your move, be careful to cast your successes in the light of the team's performance.

"You should be talking informally to your boss regularly," says Zimmerman. "Over coffee, you mention how well the team is responding to the challenges and the results they are seeing, with the emphasis always on the team, not on you individually."

Use these conversations to set up next steps. For example, if your team has learned valuable lessons that could provide benefits to other areas in your supervisor's domain, offer to facilitate some cross-team learning. This kind of proactive approach delivers short-term value and shows your commitment to the organization.

What you take away from Andrus's story and how you apply the advice of the experts, only you can determine. But almost everyone should be able to pull at least a small lesson from this observation: "A lot of executives are sitting around waiting for the next shoe to drop," Zimmerman notes. "Worse, many have buried their heads in the sand like ostriches. When you do that, another part of your anatomy is uncovered."

Reprint U0306B

Timeless Insights on How to Manage Your Time

◈　　◈　　◈

Jim Billington

The beginning of a new year is, for obvious reasons, prime selling time for the makers of desktop calendars, personal planners, and electronic organizers. But how much of an investment do you need to make in such technology? Maybe less than you think, say the experts. The best thinking on time management suggests that while you may not want to throw out these nifty devices, they certainly shouldn't be your main concern on this front. Using your time well involves priorities more than planners, focus more than frenetic activity.

Books on how to manage your time are a hardy perennial, and another author who has gardened his way onto the best-seller list is Stephen Covey, with *First Things First.* To summarize his philosophy, which recapitulates some of the classic learning on the subject: "The main thing is to keep the main thing the main thing." One hears echoes of what Peter Drucker wrote 30 years ago in *The Effective Executive:* "Doing the right thing is more important than doing things right."

Despite such wisdom, there's still too much literature on time management that puts the stress on how you can do more things faster—essentially how to manage a to-do list. This strain of thinking feeds sales of planners and organizers, often resulting in expensive paperweights and exhausted managers. There must be a better way— and, in fact, there is. We've surveyed the literature on the subject and even attended a Covey seminar, and, in the interest of saving you, well, you know what, have distilled what seem to us a few critical insights.

Begin on the Balcony

When launching any important piece of work, visualize the end result. Conceive in as much detail as possible the desired outcome of your individual effort, or that of your team. If it helps, think in terms of what Ronald A. Heifetz, coauthor of "The Work of Leadership" in the *Harvard Business Review*, calls "getting on the balcony"— seeing the whole field of play and where your undertaking should fit in. You almost certainly want to consult others as you do such imagining, particularly the people to whom you report. If you and your boss are looking for different outcomes, no amount of efficiency on your part will make up for this confusion; indeed, you might just end up digging yourself into a hole faster.

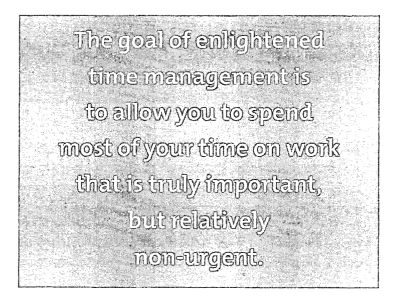

The goal of enlightened time management is to allow you to spend most of your time on work that is truly important, but relatively non-urgent.

Mission statements have a somewhat checkered reputation these days. But they can help keep your short- and medium-term projects in line with your long-range goals. Covey recommends creating personal and professional mission statements and then checking what you do every week against them. In crafting such statements, use the familiar principle of the tombstone: Set goals that you would like to see memorialized at the end of your life, as a summary of your professional and personal existence.

If the Work Is Not Necessary to Do, It's Necessary to Not Do It

It's a chestnut, but true: Your time is precious. Moreover, your talents are too important to waste on work that does not directly contribute to the mission of your organization or your personal life. In *7 Survival Skills for a Reengineered World,* William Yeomans suggests that the most helpful way of sorting out what's necessary is to think through all your decisions and actions in terms of what effect they will have upon your customers. And take a broad view of who your customers are—not just the people you sell to, your colleagues, or your boss, but your loved ones and friends as well.

Overcome the Addiction to Urgency

Most people spend most of their time at work doing things that are urgent but relatively unimportant. Fighting fires, fielding calls, firing off memos, attending irrelevant meetings—all can consume a manager's day but add little lasting value. These activities have an appealing urgency but lack importance. The addiction to busyness comes in part from a lack of self-esteem, the experts say—if I'm this overscheduled, I must be important—and in part from the popular, industrial-age misconception that work must be frenetic to be effective. (Did you ever see Charlie Chaplin in *Modern Times*?)

An engineer will tell you that work is defined as directed force times motion. All the motion in the world will not produce work if it is not coupled with direction. So it is with our professional lives. The goal of enlightened time management is to allow you to spend most of your time on work that is truly important, but relatively non-urgent.

One of the very practical ways of focusing on key work is to appropriate some time each day in which you are off-limits to phones and other interruptions. During this time, work on your top priority task. Move into another office if necessary. But do not leave unless you are needed in a genuine emergency. Try to schedule this "appointment with yourself" at a time in the day that corresponds to your biological "prime time"—whether you're a morning person or a night owl, give yourself an hour during your peak energy period to work on your most important activity.

You will also diminish the urgency addiction by under-scheduling yourself. Our authors agree that only about half of one's time ought to be scheduled. The other half ought to remain open to the needs of the day and allow for interruptions of scheduled time to attend to these needs.

Balance the Different Sectors of Your Life

Time management is not about work alone. As with work, much leisure time is wasted—devoted to activities that don't help you fulfill your personal mission. For example, watching television might be an antidote to the pressures of the office, but may do little to further your goal of being a good spouse and parent. Apply the same exercises that you use to improve the way you spend time at work to your personal life as well—a weekly check on "How am I doing against my personal statement?"

Lest you fear that we're veering into the philosophical ozone, we conclude with six handy, if not altogether unfamiliar, tips gleaned from our readings on how you can boost your efficiency once you have chosen the work that's important for you to do:

1. Don't interrupt your work when the mail comes.

2. If a piece of paper calls for action, act then—don't deal with the same piece of paper twice.

3. Screen your phone calls.

4. Consolidate call-backs and visitor time.

5. At the end of the week, throw out the "FYIs" you've collected.

6. Avoid meetings with more than 12 participants. Nothing will be accomplished.

And keep in mind another question to ask yourself daily: "What one thing can I do today that will make my life better tomorrow?"

For Further Reading

First Things First by Stephen R. Covey (1994, Simon & Schuster)

The Organized Executive: A Program for Productivity by Stephanie Winston (1994, Warner Books)

"Salvaging Sales Scrap Time" by Rebecca Morgan (*American Salesman,* October 1996, National Research Bureau, Information Access Co.)

7 Survival Skills for a Reengineered World by William N. Yeomans (1996, A Dutton Book, The Penguin Group)

Time Management for Dummies by Jeffrey J. Mayer (1995, IDG Books)

"The Work of Leadership" by Ronald A. Heifetz and Donald L. Laurie (*Harvard Business Review,* December 2001)

Reprint U9702B

Getting Organized

●   ●   ●

Constantine von Hoffman

There are moments that serve as a test of how well organized your office is:

- The boss calls, asking for a particular piece of information from a project completed a year ago. (How long does it take you to find it?)

- You've been promoted and must hand off your files to Mr. or Ms. Successor. (How much do you dread the hand-off?)

∘ You must find a phone number, a piece of paper, or a file. (How much time does it take?)

For some people, it takes three minutes to dig up the project information; the hand-off is not at all dreadful; and locating phone numbers, files, etc. takes very little time at all. Then there are the rest of us.

As is the case in much of management (and life), there is no one-size-fits-all prescription for organizing oneself. Disorganization is a highly individual matter. Some of us have found, for example, that clutter has its uses. Says Margot Honig, a professional organizer who runs Strategic Organizing Solutions in Brookline, Massachusetts, "Some people use clutter as armor against being exposed to the world." Others would like to be organized but don't know how. Still others refuse to acknowledge that it takes time and work to be organized—and even more time and work to be disorganized. Indeed, disorganization eats up work time and productivity. According to a study commissioned by the temporary employment firm Accountemps, executives waste about five weeks a year looking for lost items.

Honig and other experts say it doesn't matter what organizing system you use as long as it works for you. How you think determines whether or not a system will be comfortable. If you enjoy working on your computer and like everything electronic, use an electronic organizer. If you've been through one too many PC crashes and like information you can touch, a paper system will more likely make you happy.

A Role for Ruthlessness

Beyond that, being organized is largely a matter of managing time, paper, and space. The best way to manage disorganization is to ruthlessly eliminate what you don't need to have around. Stephanie Denton, a professional organizer in Cincinnati who's also a member of the board of the National Association of Professional Organizers, suggests applying a basic rule: The less you have, the less you have to sort through. If you feel you can't let go, visualize the senior executive who was Denton's client: He filled several giant wheeled trash hampers with papers he no longer needed.

It's helpful to think of self-organization as a kind of office hygiene, something you should do as regularly as brushing your teeth. Felicia Rand, a senior manager of information systems at an international nonprofit healthcare agency, says, "Organization is something you have to do every day." If allocating periods to straighten things up seems like a low-level priority, Rand suggests keeping track of the amount of time you lose looking for information you know you have (somewhere)—or the number of times you put off a colleague because you can't find that piece of paper she needs to get her work done.

Since it takes time to manage clutter, Rand and others suggest some basic tactics for finding the time to be organized. Take five minutes before each hour to sort and put things away. Set the clock on your computer to remind you. Or make sure to allot time at the end of each work session on a project or task to put things away and attend to whatever's been piling up. Or schedule time at the beginning or end of each day to get things in order. (This last suggestion relies on a basic truth of organizational life: The hardest time to get your work done is during the day, when everyone else is at the office, too.)

An Alternative to "Pile Management"

There are also some "space management" tactics that will support you in your drive to be more organized. If you engage in what's known as pile management—everything on your desktop is in a series of piles, all of which you keep meaning to get around to—your desk should be long rather than deep. A deep desk encourages you to put more and more piles farther back, and gives you plenty of room to keep adding files. A narrower desk encourages you to keep necessary items—and necessary items only—at your fingertips. Denton recommends an L- or U-shaped desk because it can give you specific areas in which to do different kinds of work. "A lot of people think piles alert them to what needs to be done," says

Denton, "but they don't. They just distract you from what needs to be done."

The organizing experts go so far as to suggest that those of us who manage multimillion-dollar products, scores and scores of people, and important institutions do not know what a desk is for. A desk, they tell us, is a workspace. It should hold our work tools—phone, pens, computer, calendar, in box, out box, and maybe a hanging file for items that require our action or the action of another—and whatever we're working on at the moment. A desk is not "an unregulated storage area," and using it as such guarantees that we will lose things.

Organization for Team Members and Other People

The true test of the organized manager is the ease with which he or she coordinates with other people. For that, Rand all but insists that managers and professionals rely on an online calendar, which lets people see when colleagues and team members are busy and expedites the scheduling of meetings. Posting one's whereabouts for all the world to see does, of course, give new meaning to the phrase "open-book management," but productivity seems to have little in common with privacy. Or privilege: Rand believes that online calendars work best when senior management uses them, too. Rand estimates her own online calendar cuts the amount of time she spends scheduling things by 75 percent. She sets aside two brief periods each week to transfer all changes between her personal calendar and her online calendar.

The type of calendar system you use—electronic organizer, DayRunner, Filofax, Franklin Planner—is less important than is using it consistently. It should be the modern-day manager's repository for everything. Clutterbugs who have discovered the joys of Post-it Notes in all their variable sizes and colors must, say the experts, give them up. Little scraps of paper upon which are written important numbers, appointment times, and dates invariably get lost or mis-stuck. Even if they don't, they must still be managed. Rand says the most important thing after her calendar is the software that lets her manage her to-do list, keeping it up-to-date, alerting her as deadlines or start times approach, and carrying over items that haven't been completed.

What to Do and When

Managing the "to do" list is a subject of serious attention in time management courses. Here is a more abbreviated set of tips: Write whatever you must do on one master list. Then figure out what needs to be done when, and transfer it to a daily list (a task that can be quite easily accomplished on computer calendars). Set aside a few minutes at the end of each day to go over the list and rank the priority of tasks and goals. Some people use an A-B-C method when assigning priorities ("A" for top priority; "B" for important, but not essential; "C" for things they'd like to get done but don't have to just yet).

Within the categories of A, B, and C priorities, number tasks in the order in which they must be accomplished. Be sure to think through the interim steps that lead up to the result you seek. You may have to do a lot of groundwork before you can tackle goal No. 1. And be careful to distinguish between what is urgent and what is important. What someone else is pressing you to do may not be what you need to attend to first.

The Lost Art of Filing

The most trying task for managers of the downsized organization may be filing, a skill that may be vanishing along with the personal secretary. The guiding principle in filing is to think "access." "Filing is about retrieval, not storage," Rand says. "When you create files ask yourself, 'What would I look under to find this later?'"

When creating or overhauling a filing system, determine the main categories of your work and how you think about it. Do you think in terms of project? Person? Deadlines? Then figure out what you need to keep. Remember Denton's rule: The less you have, the less you have to sort through. Some useful criteria for keeping a document:

- The information it contains can't be easily found elsewhere.

- The information it contains helps you reach a goal.

- It's been reduced or consolidated as much as possible.

- It's up-to-date.

As anyone who has ever sorted through his e-mail archives to find a file would agree, files of all kinds should be purged periodically. If you need to hold on to a lot of older records, find a spot for archival materials that's well away from where you actually work.

Finally, step back and assess your most critical needs. Organizing, says Felicia Rand, "is not just having the right papers in the right place, but understanding your priorities." There is a strategic element in being organized, one that involves knowing what you're having trouble accomplishing. Says Denton, "It all depends on what your goal is. What's costing you most dearly in terms of lost resources? Look for that first."

And if that doesn't help, consider locating help through the National Association of Professional Organizers (phone 512-206-0151, Web site http://www.ccsi.com/ ~asmi/GROUPS/NAPO). But in the absence of a personal secretary, you will still have to learn to organize yourself, since getting organized is not a job someone else can do for you. Notes Honig, "Some people want me to do it for them. It never works."

***

For Further Reading

Organize Your Office: Simple Routines for Managing Your Workspace by Ronni Eisenberg with Kate Kelly (1994, Hyperion Books)

The Complete Idiot's Guide to Organizing Your Life by Georgene Lockwood (1997, Alpha Books)

Organizing for the Creative Person by Dorothy Lehmkuhl and Dolores Cotter Lamping (1994, Crown Books)

Reprint U9801D

Tackling Specific Time- Management Challenges

o   o   o

A plethora of forces—including endless meetings, a flood of messages, "information overload," and "task overload"—conspire to steal time away from already time-starved managers. The articles in this section contain potent suggestions for tackling each one of the forces named above.

You'll discover how to make every meeting you lead or attend live up to its potential for your company, and how to process and respond to messages (especially e-mail) in ways that free up rather than consume time. In these selections, you'll also find advice on coping with all those journals, newsletters, and other information sources you have to digest in order to stay current in your job and your industry. Finally, you'll see how the savviest managers avoid task overload and prevent distractions and interruptions from derailing them.

How to Make Every Meeting Matter

○   ○   ○

Tom Krattenmaker

Terrence, the communications director of a health services company, grumbles about all the meetings he attends. When asked his job title, he quips: "Professional meeting attender." The meetings strain has grown worse since staff cuts increased his workload and that of his reports. Yet when the senior management team made a decision on his turf, Terrence was furious about *not* being invited to the meeting at which the matter was discussed.

His behavior is not as inconsistent as it may appear. Terrence's problem with meetings is that most he attends are inefficient, unfocused time drains. Worse yet is that the meetings where the company's real business gets accomplished are not managed with sufficient skill to ensure that the right players are there.

Terrence's dilemma is a common one. At a time when changes in the workplace are increasing the number of meetings held, time-starved managers and their staff members—some of them performing work once handled by two people—can afford less than ever to waste their time in meetings.

"The biggest complaints I hear about meetings are that they're unproductive, that they last too long, that they're unnecessary," says Frances A. Micale, consultant and trainer, and the author of *Not Another Meeting! A Practical Guide for Facilitating Effective Meetings* (Oasis, 2002).

"Yet at their best, meetings can mean everything to an organization," she says. "If you can consistently have good, productive meetings, your company is going to perform better. I don't think a lot of people think of it this way, but better meetings mean better communication and better decisions, and that's going to have a direct impact on the bottom line."

The Value—and the Cost—of Meetings

If you think you and your colleagues are attending more meetings than ever before, it's probably not your imagination. In the old command-and-control days, people did not need to gather in meeting rooms that often. But as the workplace has become more collaborative and democratic, experts say, organizations have needed more meetings to share information, receive people's input, and make group decisions. Moreover, mergers and alliances have increased the need for more interorganization meetings in addition to those taking place within companies.

But while meetings "at their best" can make crucial contributions to your company's success, keep in mind that meetings at their worst represent not only a lost opportunity but also wasted money. Time is finite; when one factors in the hours employees fritter away at meetings instead of using the time to complete work at their desks and in the field, companies are wasting enormous amounts of money.

The Web site EffectiveMeetings.com, operated by SMART Technologies, offers a meetings cost calculator that can help you determine the cost of meetings based on a set of variables. For example, the typical weekly management team meeting can cost a work group $390 each time it assembles—or more than $20,000 a year—assuming that the group consists of five members averaging $70,000 a year in salary and that the meetings last about two hours. Add to that dollar amount the toll taken by the accumulated stress and discontent of staffers who return from back-to-back-to-back meetings to an avalanche of messages and a deferred to-do list that grows by the day.

"I have clients telling me they are completely over-whelmed by this 'meeting mania' happening at many companies," says consultant Peggy Klaus. "In this new meeting culture, managers sometimes feel they have to hear everyone's input before they make a decision. But it can become such a time drain that it's ridiculous."

Here are some practical ideas for managers intent on having meetings that enhance, rather than hinder, their organization's success.

Don't Always Have a Meeting

The solution to an unproductive meeting might be as simple as not having it. As Klaus and other experts explain, "meeting mania" is fueled in large part by the use of meetings to take care of business better handled by other means. Before calling the troops together yet again, managers should ask themselves whether the purpose of the meeting might be fulfilled some other way. If the point is to share information—which is all too frequently the case in organizations plagued by bad meetings—e-mail, memos, and informal conversations will probably work better.

"The question is: Why have a meeting? Most people don't think through that clearly enough," says Barbara Streibel, a consultant at Oriel and author of *The Manager's Guide to Effective Meetings* (McGraw-Hill, 2002). "The best reason to have a meeting is that you really need interaction between the people who are attending. You need people to share opinions and knowledge, and build a common integrated thought-line about the issue at hand. Then a meeting—if done well—is perfect for that."

In a few cases, information sharing might also be a legitimate purpose for scheduling a meeting, says Streibel—but only if you need the immediate spontaneous give-and-take that's possible when everyone is together in real time. Otherwise, e-mail or voice mail will probably suffice.

At their worst, meetings represent lost opportunity—and they waste money.

Sometimes, curing "meeting mania" requires a shift in how you approach management, Klaus says. While a more democratic workplace is no doubt better for everyone, it does not mean that group decisions are required for all the small questions that make up a day. Micromanagers who want to vet their reports' every move are going to need more meetings. On the other hand, effectively delegating work to qualified staff members greatly relieves the need for meetings. "If I have delegated well, I won't need to be there for every decision the team is making. I'll know that Tom or Susan has taken care of things," Klaus says.

"Before calling a meeting, you've really got to ask yourself, 'What is the point?'" says Klaus. "What is it that, when you're done, you want people to do or think or feel? Ask yourself: 'Do I really *have* to have this meeting?'"

Don't "Discuss"

"Discussion" is no longer good enough. Time-starved staffs need more than directionless chatter or meant-to-impress progress reports. Productive meetings depend on clearly defined objectives toward which people can work and against which they can measure progress. "If I'm organizing a meeting, I want to get beyond 'discuss,'" Streibel says. "Maybe 'discuss and decide.' Or 'discuss and build a plan,' or 'discuss and identify key barriers to success.' I want an action. I don't need a laundry list of what's happened in the last week."

For example, if your weekly get-together with your staff members has become the bane of your existence and theirs, insist that everyone—yourself included—pares down her reports to actionable issues. Reserve the meeting "table" for items that require the whole group's thinking and action.

Spend Time to Save Time

Terrence from the first example in this article would not have missed the one meeting he did care about—and where his presence would have been most beneficial—if his company better prepared for and communicated about meetings. If the president's executive assistant had thought through and prepared a good agenda for the weekly senior staff meeting, it might have occurred to her that a wise decision on the proposed community newsletter would require Terrence's presence. (It turns out he had cost figures and survey results that would have compelled the opposite decision.)

> Deal with off-topic ideas by placing them in a "parking lot"—a real or figurative white board listing thoughts and ideas that can be pursued (or not) at a more appropriate time.

Even if she had forgotten to invite Terrence, if she routinely circulated the agenda in advance to all managers, Terrence would have known what was coming. Then he could have lobbied to join the meeting, or at least sent an e-mail to his boss with the vital information.

As a rule of thumb, Streibel suggests spending 30 to 60 minutes preparing for meetings you are responsible for organizing and/or leading. Distribute a precise, time-conscious agenda and assemble the right people. And allow participants to depart when the meeting turns to affairs not relevant to their portfolios.

Thorough advance work can produce a surprising, and welcome, decision. "By identifying the desired outcome and preparing an agenda ahead of time," the trainer and consultant Micale says, "you may realize you don't even need a meeting."

Park Digressions, Deflate Windbags

Effective meeting facilitation is a subject unto itself, but experts point to several simple concepts that will make meetings as productive—and brief—as possible. A driver who meanders off course will take longer to reach his destination than one who heads directly from A to B. The same applies to meetings, which often take far longer than necessary because participants digress.

Klaus and other experts suggest one useful and diplomatic way of steering the meeting quickly back on course without hurting any feelings: Deal with off-topic ideas by placing them in a "parking lot"—a real or figurative white board listing thoughts and ideas that can be pursued (or not) at a more appropriate time.

Pontificators and windbags can also sabotage a meeting's success even if they stay on agenda. Not only do they eat up time but they also can crowd out less loquacious participants who may have the best ideas. Polite interruptions by the meeting leader might be necessary to cut wordy monologues short. That, when combined with prompts to reluctant speakers, can keep everyone involved, which can only mean a better meeting.

At some meetings, everyone seems to want five or 10 minutes of marginally worthwhile airtime, Streibel notes. If that's the custom at your meetings, break people of the habit. "If you indulge them all and you have 10 people at a meeting," Streibel says, "you've just blown at least an hour."

Declare a Meeting-Free Day

Some companies are declaring meeting-free days. Others are making certain hours of the day off-limits for meetings. At some organizations, meetings creep is being fought through use of "stand-ups"—brief huddles where participants work through lean-mean agendas in rapid-fire fashion, literally standing up all the while to remind one another that the meeting is no time to lean back and settle in.

Streibel's advice: Use meetings sparingly, and use them well. "I know people often feel that meetings are a waste of time," she says. "But when meetings are at their best, they're a place where people can be creative together, where they can integrate everyone's perspective and knowledge and experience. So they can be an important part of a process of coming up with innovative solutions to problems and new and better ways of doing things. Who wouldn't want that?"

Reprint C0305C

Managing
Message Overload

o   o   o

Dwight Moore

A man I'll call Al Monroe is senior regional general manager of a big railroad. Commuting to work on a typical day, he uses his cell phone to take care of his 15 or so voice mails. When he arrives at the office he finds between 70 and 100 e-mails waiting. About half of these, he estimates, are irrelevant to his job. Another quarter should have gone to his direct reports. Some of the rest are interesting but need no action; others are ambiguous. Only about 5% require him to do something right away. Still, reading and responding to messages takes all of his commute plus most of his first two hours at work.

Sound familiar?

By now, even senior executives in most organizations have come to expect an overload of messages every day. But few of us have come to terms with the implications of this deluge for the way we work.

Think about it. Most communications in today's electronic world are one-way rather than interactive. Voice mail and e-mail messages are short, didactic, monosyllabic, operational, and detailed. Since the sender generally expects a response, they create a sense of urgency. We leap to answer our messages before we do anything else.

Then, too, the new technologies have made it possible for companies to eliminate many secretarial positions. A manager equipped with voice mail doesn't need someone to answer her calls; one with e-mail doesn't need to have many letters typed up. So executives find themselves screening calls, arranging meetings on their electronic calendars, and reading dozens of messages that don't really concern them.

But the most dangerous consequence of these media is that they drive planning, thinking, and decision making to the micro level. They focus a manager's attention squarely on details to the exclusion of big-picture concerns. Consider your own e-mails. They probably deal with matters such as meetings, fires that need to be put out, requests from your boss or direct reports, and so on. They probably don't focus on strategic matters or any other longer-term objectives.

Al Monroe's situation illustrates the danger. When asked what his annual goals were, he cited three objectives that vitally affected his company's long-range profitability. One of them involved a shortage of locomotives: in a booming economy, engines couldn't be built fast enough to meet demand. But when asked what he had done to address this issue, he paused, and admitted he hadn't visited it recently. He hadn't had time.

Four Steps to Message Control

If this pretty much describes your situation, it's time for action. You need to rearrange your priorities and manage your messages. I recommend four steps.

1: Begin Your Day Differently

Instead of jumping to your e-mail, start the day with a blank piece of paper. Write down a strategic goal and develop an operational plan to tackle what needs to be done first (or next). Allocate a block of uninterrupted time to work on that goal.

2: Do E-Mails at the End of the Day

You're tired then, and eager to get home. You'll be better at focusing on the important ones and keeping your responses short. Besides, fewer people will be able to respond immediately.

3: Teach People How to Send You E-Mails

One executive decided to respond to every e-mail for a week with a note on its appropriateness. He coded his responses: a 1 meant, Keep sending this sort of critical information; 2, Unless I'm on this team, don't send me this information; 3, Send this to the responsible person on my staff, not to me; and so on. His e-mail load dropped precipitously.

4: Teach Your Boss Not to Micromanage You with E-Mail

If he asks for a piece of information that's handled by your staff, refer him to the appropriate person. And don't feel obliged to answer every small request right away. Rather, be sure to keep the boss informed of the big-picture activities you're choosing to attend to instead.

Finally, remember that nothing other than threats to life is all that urgent. Take time to breathe. Establish priorities for your work. Make a point of relying on face-to-face meetings, not messages, for anything that involves ambiguity, interaction, or emotion. Technology is only a tool, and it shouldn't determine how we make decisions, how we manage our time, or how relaxed we feel.

Reprint U9911D

Coping with Infoglut

Learn from the Folks in Financial Services

❁   ❁   ❁

Edward Prewitt

As you read this book, think of all the other publications you need to peruse this week: the magazines, the journals, the newspapers. Think of the letters, the memos, the reports, and the faxes spooling out of the machine, the e-mail, the Webcast, and the corporate intranet display clamoring for attention. Better yet, try not to think about it all. Information overload—dubbed Information Fatigue Syndrome—can actually harm your health, at least according to a 1996 report sponsored by Reuters Business Information. More than 40% of senior managers and a third of all managers (of 1,300 surveyed around the world) reported ill health as a direct consequence of stress associated with information overload.

"Data smog," as the title of a popular book has it, seems to be getting worse, not better. The Internet threatens to turn information flow into a tidal wave. Nowhere is this quandary more apparent, and more threatening, than in financial services. For bankers, fund managers, investment managers, analysts, and traders, the true currency is information, not cash.

Harvard psychology professor Daniel Gilbert notes that information overload impairs the brain's ability to perform tasks like analysis and decision making. What a catch-22 for financial professionals, who daily must dissect and act on huge quantities of information. How do they keep up? "Black magic," jokes Arieh Coll, portfolio manager of Fidelity Investment's Trend Fund. Yet some survive and even prosper. From managers in different segments of financial services, here are techniques and tools.

Prioritize

"Very few people are overloaded by critical information," says Gilbert. "There's a lot of information out there, some of it critical, but 90% of it useless, probably." Prioritization is your first task. Matthew Robertson, who manages a portfolio of international bonds at Neuberger & Berman, LLC, has narrowed his A list of daily information sources down to six people—three fixed-income brokers and three currency traders—and two computer screens on Reuters and Bloomberg terminals, each one a composite screen he set up from the thousands of options that both services offer. At Fidelity, Coll separates the two feet of mail that arrives at his office every day into five in-boxes—one each for material from companies he follows, reports on international markets, brokerage analyses, prospectuses, and faxes. His reading begins with the first two. "Not all information gets treated equally," he says.

Filter Information Sources

A necessity, our authorities agree, is setting limits on the quantity of information arriving. This may seem counterintuitive for people who are always seeking that extra nugget of info that might give them a competitive edge. As Coll puts it, "You force happy accidents by maximizing the amount of information you take in." But since the volume of verbiage written on almost any industry or portfolio of companies is too much to keep up with, he and others say it's important to filter out the less useful sources of information and home in on the richer veins. "There's a proliferation these days. There's more crap that comes through the door," says money manager Scott Black, president of Delphi Management. "We try to separate the scatter from the signal—that's the key thing." To track companies he already invests in, Black reads only the company reports, company faxes announcing important news, and earnings digests. To keep a lookout for new companies to invest in, Delphi created a mathematical model to perform a first screen of company financials. "We gave a lot of thought to the formal criteria" of the mathematical model, Black says. "It saves 99% of our time."

Lessen or Eliminate Lesser Sources

Just because others read certain publications doesn't mean you should. For many of our managers, daily newspapers and general business magazines simply aren't useful. "I spend less time reading general newspapers these days. The higher-quality info tends to be in the more focused publications," says investment banker Peter Stalker, a partner at E. M. Warburg, Pincus & Company. "And the 'business lite' publications—*Fortune, Forbes,* and *Business Week*—with those I spend a lot less time. I've screened down to a handful of better sources." Investment banker Michael Dauchot, an analyst at Robertson, Stephens & Company, says he rarely reads the general business press "because in my experience what they write is often inaccurate." Black reads *The Wall Street Journal* cover to cover at home at night because he finds it "intellectually interesting, but not directly related to what I need to know" for investment decisions.

One more bottom-dweller is Wall Street research reports, Coll says. "They're black holes of time. Brokerage research is public information—they don't want to offend. It's never balanced." Venture capitalist David Golob, an associate at Sutter Hill Ventures, finds equity research from investment banks "mostly useless." Another time-waster, he says, is browsing through the World Wide Web. Not that Web research is inherently profitless—"but you have to know what you're looking for fairly precisely." Yet as anyone who has spent time on the Web knows, surfing through it for links both related and random is one of its seductive pleasures. This highlights a truth about inferior information sources: Avoiding these time sinks takes conscious thought and vigilance. "It's so easy to sit down with a daily newspaper, but I've determined that's not a useful source for me," sighs Coll.

Free Yourself for Face-to-Face Conversations

Information, whatever its format, reflects the work and thought of other people. It follows that two-way conversations with those people will generally be superior. "People are interactive. Articles aren't," Coll says. "Articles have many audiences. Most aren't written for me. . . .

People are time-savers." Face-to-face conversations are such a superior information source that Coll, who follows approximately 1,000 companies, makes it a point to see executives from at least half those each year, despite the time-consuming and exhausting nature of business travel. Face-to-face is even better than phone-to-phone, says Stalker of Warburg, Pincus. "When you really need info that's specific, there's no substitute for face-to-face. The nuances of their body language and their facial expressions are lost on the phone."

Satisfice

This portmanteau word from economics, a combination of "satisfy" and "suffice," succinctly describes the necessity of cutting off research once an appropriate amount of time has resulted in a sufficient amount of useful information. "There can be a needle in a haystack—but the haystack can be too much damn trouble to look through," says Golob. Besides, points out Delphi Management's Black, "You're not going to get everything. If you strive for perfection, you'll go crazy and you'll never reach it anyway."

Do Your Own Analysis

"I'd rather get the facts and do my own analysis," says Dauchot at Robertson, Stephens. "Unless you're really an expert in a field, you don't know how accurate someone else's analysis is." Black is given to quoting Descartes: "The work of one is oftentimes better than the work of many." "There are a lot of idiots out there," adds Black, whose six-person firm has compiled an 18.5% compounded annual return over the last 17 years. "We don't want to rely on their thinking."

Outsource Work When You Can

That's not to say you have to work in solitary confinement. Intelligent, reliable analysis can be found. For example, the consulting firm Gartner Group has built a reputation for sound analysis of the information technology sector, say Stalker and Golob. "You find info sources that work for you and you stick with them," says Stalker. "I can't think of an instance where we didn't hear of something between our personal contacts and our regular sources."

Use the Internet to Tame the Internet

The newest and most prodigious information sources, the Internet and its subset, the World Wide Web, are often blamed for accelerating the infoglut to ridiculous levels. Yet the amount of *new* business information on the Internet is not that large, argue David Boghossian and Tim Duncan, who in 1994 created a Web site named the Corporate Finance Network (www.corpfinet.com) that compiles a broad range of financial data and analysis. What is so notable about the Internet, they say, is that it allows near-instant access to gigabytes of information which formerly required a great deal of time and effort to find.

In response to the fire-hose nature of the Internet, several methods of focusing online research have been invented. The most rudimentary tool is the search engine. Even so, search engines are relatively broad-brush, often responding to a query with hundreds or thousands of hits. With a second method, "push," a Web user can profile his specific information needs, allowing Web operators to send him only news and data that fit his outline. Stalker and Golob both recommend Individual (www.individual.com), which sorts and ranks stories of interest from hundreds of news sources, sending them each night to corporate Web servers. Despite their specificity, however, push sites are just one more load of information, and a particularly heavy one at that. A better alternative may be one like that offered by Boghossian and Duncan's firm, Story Street Partners. Story Street Partners uses the intranets—internal computer networks—of client financial services firms to create custom interfaces that combine news feeds, filtered Web content, and internal company information. These proprietary interfaces consolidate information sources and ensure that employees are all on the same page, so to speak.

Know Where You Want to Go

Casting a wide net is no longer an appropriate image for information-gathering; nowadays harpooning might be more apt. "It's amazing what you can find out now, if you have a mind to," says Robertson of Neuberger & Berman. "So you have to set up a strategy for what you think is important. . . . You've got to have an overall direction."

For Further Reading

Data Smog: Surviving the Information Glut by David Schenk (1997, HarperCollins)

Dying for Information? An Investigation into the Effects of Information Overload in the U.K. and Worldwide by Reuters Business Information (1996, Firefly Communications)

Reprint U9708D

Is Multitasking Overrated?

o   o   o

Jennifer McFarland

For decades, the ability to switch rapidly from one activity to the next has been assumed to be the quintessence of managerial work. Indeed, half of managers' activities last nine minutes or less, and only one-tenth of their tasks take more than an hour, notes McGill University professor Henry Mintzberg in his 1973 classic, *The Nature of Managerial Work* (Harper & Row). It stands to reason that this need to multitask would only become stronger during a downturn: as companies eliminate positions and consolidate others, there are fewer managers left to keep more plates spinning.

But how far can you push the logic of multitasking before it backfires? "Management wants to believe that somehow they can consolidate various jobs, reassign them to one person and have that person be as productive as were the three or more independent workers who performed these jobs before," says David Meyer, professor of psychology at the University of Michigan. "In most cases it just isn't possible. The brain's limitations can't be escaped."

Companies may be vastly underestimating the time costs of multitasking. Mounting evidence shows that a crowded calendar calling for a lot of jumping back and forth between activities can diminish rather than enhance productivity. A study by Meyer and his colleagues indicates that the brain goes through a kind of warm-up period whenever an individual begins a new task. "You have to get your attention focused, you have to remind yourself what the issues are," explains Meyer.

Once that's done, your mind is primed to work productively. But even a 30-second distraction can be enough to derail you, and like a boiling pot of water removed from the burner, your brain needs time to warm up again afterward. Depending on how often you're forced to switch from one task to another, the associated time costs can add up to as much as two to four hours a day, the study reveals.

A Need to Focus

As Peter Drucker has famously observed, successful management depends on doing the right things rather than doing things right. You need to identify the few activities that are most important for you to do and concentrate your efforts on them. Yet only 10% of managers have the necessary focus and energy, conclude Dr. Heike Bruch, professor of leadership at the University of St. Gallen, Switzerland, and Dr. Sumantra Ghoshal, former professor of strategy and international management at the London Business School, based on their 10-year study of busy managers. Whereas other managers give primary consideration to constraining forces—for example, bosses, peers, or job descriptions—when deciding what's feasible, effective managers work from the outside in: "They decide first what they must achieve and then work to manage the external environment," write Bruch and Ghoshal ("Beware the Busy Manager," *Harvard Business Review*, February 2002).

> A crowded calendar calling for a lot of jumping back and forth between activities can diminish rather than enhance productivity.

They also tend to be more self-aware, identifying their goals, choosing their battles, and managing their time more carefully than other managers do. "People who are committed to do something are not easily distracted," says Bruch. "They manage to get back to their intention even after interruption."

Take Multitasking Down off the Pedestal

You can't always avoid having to tend to half a dozen matters within the space of an hour, but if you continue to view such occasions as the managerial ideal instead of a necessary evil, you'll never make any improvements.

Delegate Everything That You Don't Need to Do Personally

Delegation, as it's usually presented, "makes little sense," writes Drucker in *The Effective Executive* (HarperBusiness, 1996). "If it means that somebody else ought to do part of '*my* work,' it is wrong." No manager has enough time to do all the things she considers important; the only way to even get to the important things "is by pushing on others anything that can be done by them at all."

Practice Time Blocking

Says Meyer: "Block off periods of time where you won't get interrupted and where you can go about doing the task after the warm-up that must take place." You need to be able "to dispose of time in fairly large chunks," particularly for the sustained thought and calibrated judgment required by people decisions and the process of innovation, writes Drucker. "To have small dribs and drabs of time at [your] disposal will not be sufficient even if the total is an impressive number of hours."

Reprint U0206D

Making Smarter Decisions Faster

o   o   ⊙

It's no surprise that most managers feel they have less time than ever to accomplish more work than before. As the pace of business quickens, managers everywhere have come under pressure to make smarter decisions with little time and inadequate information. If you've just started a new job at a struggling company, the need to act fast is even more urgent.

Though making smarter decisions faster may sound impossibly difficult, there *are* tactics you can use to quicken your decision making while still making wise choices. The selections that follow are packed with strategies—including using prototypes to hand decision making over to customers; seizing opportunities to advance your knowledge so you can draw on it quickly when needed; and sidestepping common cognitive pitfalls, such as the "sunk-cost" trap.

Fast-Cycle
Decision Making

Edward Prewitt

Over the last decade, many companies, even entire industries, have embraced fast-cycle techniques as a means of radically speeding up production and product development. But for all its benefits, the focus on speed has often made managers' jobs more difficult. Rapidly changing markets have rendered forecasting, planning, and organizing—the bedrock tasks of management—hurried and perilously uncertain.

How do you plan inventory for the next quarter when the book of business changes weekly? How do you focus the product-development program when the market could make your efforts obsolete overnight? In short, how do you make good business decisions when your business changes so fast?

Add a new arrow to the managerial quiver: fast-cycle decision making. Fast-cycle decision making is accomplished not by simply "pedaling faster," but by systematically changing the way your team processes information. Here are tips from leading management thinkers and companies to help you hone your ability to act wisely, even in the face of insufficient time and inadequate data.

1: Rethink the Decision Model

The standard model of market research—a time-intensive effort to gather as much data as possible and then synthesize it—has always been somewhat unsatisfactory, since "perfect information" is a chimera. But the need for speed shatters this traditional decision construct. Markets move so fast that a manager waiting for extensive information risks leaving the gate too late. Asea Brown Boveri (ABB) CEO Percy Barnevik understood this new reality when he formulated his "7-3 formula" in the late 1980s: it's better to make a decision quickly and be right seven times out of ten than to delay while searching for the perfect solution, he told his managers. Accepting such a high rate of error "may seem horrendous at first, but when you think about it a little further, a fast decision gives you options that a slow decision doesn't," says Rensselaer Polytechnic Institute professor emeritus Walter Reitman, a management and decision sciences expert. "If you make the decision quickly, and it turns out in a week or two or three to have difficulties nobody anticipated, you stand a pretty good chance of being able to reverse it or modify it and still be in time to deal with the market problems." Conversely, a decision delayed is a decision forgone. Barnevik's mantra is a cornerstone of ABB's success: "Better roughly and quickly than carefully and slowly. The only thing we cannot accept is people who do nothing."

How do you ensure that your decisions turn out right at least 70% of the time? By relying on managerial intuition, answers Paul Magill, senior consultant at Monitor Company. Intuition may seem, at first, to be a slippery slope on which to base business judgments, but it's actually a reliable way to tap into managers' accumulated know-how. "People who are good intuitive decision makers are leveraging their knowledge," says Magill. Intuition also fits the ideal of fast decision making, he adds: "It's insightful, creative, and not gated by months and months of analysis."

2: Interconnect

Real-time electronic collaboration is so new that many companies have yet to grasp how it can revolutionize decision making. Communications technology today "is focused on compressing to zero the amount of time it takes to acquire and use information, to learn, to make decisions, to initiate action, to deploy resources, to innovate," notes Regis McKenna in his book *Real Time.* Such time compression is effected not by linking one manager to all sources of information—a data glut can be as deadly as the lack of data—but by linking many managers to one another. By taking advantage of the connectivity born of e-mail, the Internet and World Wide Web, and information-sharing software such as Lotus Notes, managers can merge their knowledge bases and decision-making capabilities to consider problems faster and at an earlier stage than was previously possible. "Store-and-forward technology . . . allows people in organizations to get involved in a larger number of things—not making decisions on them, necessarily, but offering an opinion or routing it to somebody else," says Christopher Meyer, director of Ernst & Young's Center for Business Innovation. "Issues take shape as opinions get knocked up against one another. People are touching more and more streams of thought."

This collaboration changes more than just the speed with which decisions are made; it changes *how* they are made. "Certain issues can even solve themselves, because by wandering around among different thinkers, they take a shape which becomes a decision," adds Meyer, who calls this process "intramural decision making."

3: Market-Test

Traditionally viewed as the ultimate pass-fail test for products, the market can sometimes be used for early-stage testing and feedback. Netscape routinely places beta versions of its software—bugs and all—on the Web, attracting testers by offering the products for free. This procedure in effect hands much decision-making power over to the potential customers. "Putting a prototype in the market and getting a reaction and letting the market shape it, even to the point of identifying the bugs and in some cases suggesting fixes . . . accelerates your decision making so you're responding to market information first rather than at the end of the decision cycle," Meyer explains. "Let the market manage your product" is a major theme of the book, *Blur,* that Meyer coauthored.

Amazon.com takes this concept even further. Seeking customer feedback at every opportunity, the online bookseller is able to learn about buyer preferences very quickly. As a result, Amazon stocks books at optimal levels, hones the way it packages its offerings, and reaches both repeat customers and potential patrons in new and unexpected ways. "Amazon seems to bring out a new 'wrinkle' with enormous frequency, by cycling through what the market's telling them and responding to it," Meyer says.

Although the instant connectivity engendered by the Web gives virtual companies like Netscape and Amazon a speed advantage, manufacturers and service firms can also use the Internet to move decision making closer to customers. Dell Computers used to rely on the telephone to sell directly to customers. On the Web, however, Dell is able to give its clientele far more information about purchase options at the same time that it tracks their preferences. This online capability has allowed Dell to lower its delivery time from 14 days to 2.

4: Redesign the Decision Process

Just as manufacturing operations can be redesigned to reduce process time, a decision-making process can be reformulated to reach a resolution faster, observes Monitor Company director Doug Rohall. He helps corporate clients identify the critical choices they face by quizzing them about the market landscape in which they operate; he then helps them narrow their focus to the few items that require the most immediate attention, such as process operations or the company's pricing strategy. "Essentially, we're honing the question, 'designing the spec,'" Rohall says. This approach is particularly helpful for situations involving a great deal of uncertainty, such as new-product launches where customer needs are poorly understood, or market moves for which it's next to impossible to predict competitors' reaction. Next, Rohall helps executives determine how they can go about learning what they need to know. "Say it's really hard to think about the competitive reaction, but it's easier to go talk to 50 customers. Then do that first," Rohall recommends. His method also highlights areas where certainty is impossible: "Not everything can be quantified well. The task is to bound choices as rigorously as possible."

Magill applies a similar systematization to his clients' strategic decision making. He studies the competitive context in which they operate: the industry segments, customers, competitors, employees, product development, operations, marketing, pricing, distribution channels, partners, and regulators. "One of the most helpful things a manager can do is understand the full range of strategic issues," he declares. Frequently, this systematic review exposes managerial blind spots. For instance, Magill explains, "some managers are fixated on what the customer just told them. Other people get fixated on capacity utilization, because they crunch the numbers and know that that's what drives profitability. Both are correct, but when they are faced with a strategic decision that has to be made, they can't integrate these concerns."

5: Decentralize Decision Making

Although pushing decision-making authority down the hierarchy to lower-level and middle managers is increasingly widespread, this precondition of fast-cycle decision making should not be overlooked. "A lot of the older decision-making structure was inherited from people who served in the military, where it was assumed that the guy underneath you was an idiot," says Reitman. Not only does that assumption run counter to the expectations of today's employees, it also wastes resources. Even the military—the classic command-and-control organization—is catching on to the advantages of empowered employees: Meyer points out that the U.S. Marines are now taught to independently assess a situation and make a decision rather than simply wait for an order.

Shorter product life cycles, streamlined product development cycles, rapidly opening (and closing) market opportunities—they all underscore the need for an overhaul of the way business decisions get made. Fast-cycle strategies help you work smarter *and* faster, reworking and rewiring your company's decision-making processes to maximum advantage.

For Further Reading

Blur: The Speed of Change in the Connected Economy by Stan Davis and Christopher Meyer (1998, Addison-Wesley)

Real Time: Preparing for the Age of the Never-Satisfied Customer by Regis McKenna (1997, Harvard Business School Press)

The Death of Distance: How the Communications Revolution Is Changing Our Lives by Frances Cairncross (2001, paperback edition, Harvard Business School Press)

Reprint U9808C

Speed Leading

Do You Have What It Takes?

o   ◌   o

**Robert J. Thomas and
Warren Bennis**

Speed is a given in today's economy, especially when you consider how quickly dangerous repercussions can be initiated by seemingly insignificant events. But the prerequisites for rapid execution—fast direction setting and decision making—often remain invisible. These skills are essentially leadership functions, but how can you tell if you or your job candidate possesses them?

Characteristics of a Speed Leader

In the research for our book *Geeks and Geezers*, we explored the qualities of 43 men and women—half of whom are under 35 years old and half of whom are over 70—who have proven their capacity to lead with speed in a remarkably broad array of situations. Geezers such as Dee Hock, CEO emeritus of Visa, and Robert Crandall, former chairman of American Airlines, have been in leadership positions for a long time and have demonstrated the ability to use more than one leadership style. For the geeks, our selection criteria were the results they've achieved and also their reputations. We chose individuals whom peers identified as people they would follow; examples here include Wendy Kopp, founder of the non-profit Teach for America, and Jeff Wilke, senior vice president of Amazon.com. Our interviews over the course of two years have yielded some important insights about leaders who prosper in high-velocity environments.

They Thrive in Unstructured Settings

Organizational theorist Karl Weick says that such environments require a compass because there are no maps, or all the relevant ones are hopelessly out of date. Business schools, like officer-training programs in the U.S. Army, have taught legions of graduates a basic leadership technique for such surroundings: the "OODA" loop, a continuous process of *observing, orienting, deciding,* and *acting.* But the leaders we interviewed exhibit a very different direction-setting approach when confronted by the messy or the unfamiliar—something we call "ALA," for *act, learn,* and *adapt.* Speed leaders experiment in order to advance knowledge. Ian Clarke, 24-year-old cofounder of the software firm Uprizer.com, describes it as constantly being on the lookout for "things you don't know you don't know." UCLA basketball coach John Wooden guided his team to an unprecedented seven consecutive national championships, but when we asked him when he felt he'd gotten the hang of coaching, he replied: "I never got the hang of it."

The ability to thrive in messiness grows out of the leader's belief that she can learn from a variety of sources. Muriel Siebert, the first woman to own a seat on the New York Stock Exchange, pressures herself to see the world from many different perspectives: her own, those of her subordinates and peers, those of her customers, creditors, and regulators. Constantly putting herself in others' shoes creates a tension—an edginess—that drives her to look for previously unseen connections.

They Lead with a Light Hand

Ask a wrestler or a tennis player what's the right stance to assume when preparing to take on an unfamiliar opponent or receive a serve. The answers you get will probably have to do with relaxation, intensity of focus, and preparedness for the unexpected. Ask a speed leader how he leads in circumstances of rapid change and you will most likely get very similar answers. Indeed, what comes to mind when you listen to Sky Dayton, who at 29 led the rapid expansion of Internet service provider

Earthlink, is the injunction that riding coaches give: ride with a light hand, neither holding onto the reins with a death grip nor letting go of them entirely and ceding control to the horse. This enables the rider to send corrections to the horse when necessary and to impart the experience of freedom when not. Case in point: Dayton knew he could release the reins at Earthlink when a CEO candidate literally talked him through a stretch of dangerous mountain driving.

Speed leaders are quick to engage the people around them in collaborative problem solving. Well-led teams, maintains Elizabeth Kao, 32-year-old global brand manager for Ford Motor Company's flagship Thunderbird program, know how to tackle problems quickly and are skilled at deciding *how* to decide—whether, for example, an issue should be resolved through consensus, via a majority vote, or by a minority that feels passionately about it.

At the same time, speed leaders can make tough decisions, resolve debates quickly, and be directive when they have to. Here, as with thriving in messiness, self-confidence plays a prominent role, but it's not the arrogance of a George Patton, nor is it a blinding conceit. Instead, it is the product of convictions deeply rooted in values whose application may be examined but whose core is unalterable. Both Dayton and Kao can make quick decisions, change the course of their teams, and demonstrate nimbleness as negotiators because their bedrock beliefs about how to treat customers—indeed, all people—provide an orienteering function: they give a sense of direction, and in so doing, help save time.

They Gain Control over the Pace and Flow of Time

Like master craftsmen, speed leaders exercise their skill with apparent effortlessness and fluidity. Like magicians, they seem capable of transcending physical constraints. And like consummate artists, they use *practice* to avoid becoming hostage to time: they learn while others are merely watching or unreflectively doing. This attribute is probably the most profound differentiator between those who succeed as speed leaders and those who fail.

Many business executives complain that they have no time to practice because they must continually perform. But the celebrated dancer and choreographer Twyla Tharp practices while she performs. She has cultivated the ability to learn and adapt in real time, often verbalizing her thoughts as a way to engage others in the process of adjustment.

V. Sundararajan, chairman and CEO of Bharat Petroleum, makes time do double duty by turning every conversation into a learning opportunity and every business challenge into a leadership lesson. Sundararajan has developed the ability to step outside the moment to see himself in action; he is able to observe the situation, reflect on his responses to it, and adjust his stance, even while remaining focused on the here and now. In four years, he has transformed his organization from little more than a cosseted, state-owned employment program into a vibrant private company that is highly profitable despite the loss of government protections.

Like a martial arts master, the speed leader is already planning her response to stimuli that others are just encountering. Constant practice has greatly enhanced her ability to anticipate what comes next. Thus, when you ask a speed leader how she knows she's gained control over time she'll probably smile. Then deny, like Coach Wooden, that she's ever gotten the hang of it.

And then leap to her next breakthrough product, decision, or idea.

_____

Reprint U0204E

Advice to Leaders
in New Jobs

Act Fast When the Economy Is Slow

○   ○   ○

Jennifer McFarland

In his first few weeks as Home Depot's new CEO in December 2000, Robert Nardelli held a three-day session with the company's officers, met with store managers in eight cities in eight days, then headed off to South America for back-to-back meetings with employees, vendors, and contractors. While spending the next few months visiting as many stores as possible, he also pushed through several senior-level hires, reassigned five executives, and eliminated a layer of management so that all the company's U.S. division presidents reported directly to him.

Why the breakneck pace? When Nardelli came on board, Home Depot was experiencing efficiency problems that often plague a company that has grown very large very fast: in January 2001, the company experienced its first quarterly earnings decline in 15 years. Still, you'd hardly describe it as a turnaround situation. Nardelli simply didn't want to have the company waiting on his learning curve.

Even in good times, there's precious little time to celebrate landing that dream job—division head, a position on the senior management team, or perhaps even CEO. You've got to hit the ground running. The impressions you make and the victories or setbacks you experience during the initial phase of your new leadership position will have a disproportionate impact on how your performance is assessed. But with the economy still sputtering, assuming the mantle of leadership now carries added significance—and attracts extra scrutiny.

Experts such as Michael Watkins, author of the online tool "Leadership Transitions" and associate professor at Harvard Business School, say you need to have people energized and focused on solving important business problems within your first six months. Others, citing Franklin Delano Roosevelt's first administration as the model, say you have 100 days to set the tone for your tenure. Obviously, your particular circumstances will play a determinative role. "If you're 26 years old and in your first leadership position—one that has a long-term career path in a large, fairly stable organization—you have more room to maneuver," says longtime Harvard Business School professor John Kotter. "But if the company's bleeding, requiring an immediate turnaround, 100 days is a big deal."

Whatever the precise time frame is, it's definitely short—and getting shorter. In his 1996 classic, *Leading Change*, Kotter notes that a major change initiative can sometimes take seven years to complete. These days, he says, you've got only about three years to pull it off. And if you're in a turnaround situation, you've got even less time: according to a Bain & Co. study of 21 business transformations over the past decade, the most successful turnarounds happen within 20 months.

But assuming that your company doesn't need organizational CPR, there are calibration issues to keep in mind even as you try to accelerate the decision making as much as you can. You can't give every project the same weight. If you enter with guns blazing, attacking on all fronts, you risk alienating important allies. Here is some advice about how to implement a fast-break philosophy without steamrolling the people you need most.

Try to Get a Leg Up

If you're coming into the leadership position from the outside, you may have a lot to learn about the company's goals and culture, its customers, and perhaps even the industry. You'll also have to build a support network. And regardless of whether you're from the inside or the

Something They Can Take to Heart

The Power of See-Feel-Change

In the years since he wrote the bestseller *Leading Change*, Harvard Business School professor John Kotter says he's developed a "greater appreciation of the limits of the analytical—and of the importance of showing people by example and touching their emotions."

"Changing people's behavior is less a matter of giving people analysis to influence their thoughts than helping them to see a truth *to influence their feelings*," Kotter writes in his book *The Heart of Change* (Harvard Business School Press, 2002). "Both thinking and feeling are essential, both are found in successful organizations, but the heart of change is in our emotions. The flow of see-feel-change is more powerful than of analysis-think-change."

Thus, the most effective short-term wins don't just serve the analytical purpose of providing "important feedback to change leaders about the validity of their

outside, and no matter how solid your reputation is, you'll still have to establish your credibility *in the new position*.

Bruce Claflin, president and CEO of 3Com, enjoyed a sterling reputation when he joined the telecommunications network equipment company in August 1998. He had been senior vice president and general manager at Digital and, before that, had spent 22 highly successful years at IBM, where he launched the Thinkpad line of laptop computers. Yet Claflin didn't believe that this visions and strategies." They serve the following emotional purposes as well:

- They "give those working hard to achieve a vision a pat on the back."
- They "build faith in the effort, attracting those who are not yet actively helping."
- They "take power away from cynics."

One example Kotter cites is of a state government's transportation department that was trying to build support for its change initiative. To win over a key state senator, who owned a trucking company, the department placed at the top of its agenda the streamlining of the 15 forms the state required trucking firms to fill out each year. The department reduced the necessary documentation to a single form, without undermining any needed government function. His pet peeve eliminated, the senator quickly became a vocal supporter of the department's initiative.

impressive track record bought him any extra time to get the lay of the land. "There's a constant debate about how fast to move the organization," he says. "Am I going too far, too fast? My belief is that almost all the time the answer is no. Whatever you're doing, do it faster. Every mistake I've made occurred when I didn't move fast enough, deep enough."

But foundation-laying work can be compressed only so much, so it helps to start on the tasks before your first day on the new job. Capitalizing on this time before entry, write Michael Watkins and Dan Ciampa in *Right from the Start*, is the key to a strong start out of the blocks. When you're not yet immersed in the day-to-day demands of the new job, you can learn a great deal about the more strategic issues facing the unit or organization you're joining.

Try to negotiate some of this transitional time with your new employer. Use it to talk to people in the organization and also to people who've left it, advises John T. Gardner, vice chairman of the recruiting firm Heidrick & Struggles. "Have an open discussion about what it's like there, what the issues are, what the organization is really good at, what it's not good at." Try to experience the company first-hand, the way a customer would. Also, spend time with your boss and, if appropriate, with your boss's boss. It's the only way to acquire a clear understanding of what's going to be expected of you and of how things get done in your group, adds Gardner.

Build Social Capital

Bill Catucci didn't have the luxury of time before entry when he became the head of Equifax's North American operations in November 1999. The North American unit, which focuses on consumer credit reporting services, represented the core business—three-quarters of total company revenue—but because it was in such dire straits, Equifax's stock was in free-fall. In the first three months,

Catucci implemented a Balanced Scorecard performance-measurement system with the help of his executive assistant, Ann Drake, a longtime Equifax employee, and overhauled the governance model.

In the new structure, Catucci and his direct reports—10 senior leaders, all of whom are on the same incentive plan—spend 12 hours together each month, convening in three distinct incarnations: a business development council, which focuses on growth; a committee that works on removing costs from key business processes; and a professional development roundtable devoted to issues of hiring, training, and compensation.

The North American unit's fortunes rebounded dramatically. The first quarter of 2000 brought the first of eight successive quarters of share-price increases for Equifax—a record unmatched in that period by any other company on the S&P 500, Catucci claims.

Catucci accomplished all this without having to replace any of the unit's senior leaders. "I was thrown right into developing a business plan—but I didn't even know the business," he recalls. "I had to rely on the top team that was in place to tell me what the relevant performance measures were. I needed to get their buy-in quickly, but I couldn't simply ram the new initiatives down their throats."

Don't Arrive with All the Answers

High personal standards and confidence—the very qualities that make you a strong candidate for leadership—

can contribute to your downfall if they lead you to believe you can do it all on your own. A common mistake is to burst upon the scene armed with financial data to support a predetermined silver-bullet answer. "New leaders fall into this trap through arrogance or insecurity or because they believe they must appear decisive and establish a direct tone," says Watkins. Of course your boss will expect you to have some ideas when you come on board. But it's hard to rally employees behind you if they think your proposals are half-baked. Instead, come prepared with a sense of what needs to be done, but allow for the fact that you still have learning to do.

After Robert A. Eckert became chairman and CEO of toy maker Mattel, he soon realized that "recognizing my own lack of knowledge about the company's people and culture—in effect, allowing employees to be the 'boss' in certain situations—actually helped me lead" ("Where Leadership Starts," *Harvard Business Review*, November 2001). Early on, Eckert sought to fill a few positions with people he'd worked with in the past. Today, he's glad he didn't railroad all these appointments through: had he not listened to the HR head's advice, he'd have ended up with some senior managers whose styles were incompatible with Mattel's culture.

"Impressions, ideas, and strong feelings about how to deal with issues"—the perspective that a network of advisers provides—"can be more important than financial analyses in making crucial early decisions," says Watkins. "Isolation is your worst enemy."

Concentrate on Short-Term Wins That Tap into People's Emotions

The goal for the initial phase of your new leadership position, Watkins believes, should be building momentum toward what you aim to accomplish over the next two to three years. But to build that momentum, "you need to give primacy to the short run," he says. Early wins create a foundation for those deeper improvements. So look for solvable problems that are strategically and symbolically significant. For example: bottlenecks that reduce productivity, a stalled hiring decision, or a poorly administered incentive program (see box, "Something They Can Take to Heart: The Power of See-Feel-Change").

"You have to get some victories so people will feel good about themselves," one leader explains in *Right from the Start*. And the developmental experiences you acquire on the job are invaluable, says Joan Gurvis, a senior program associate at the Center for Creative Leadership. "Each challenge will prepare you for the next, more difficult challenge. In effect, you're laying the foundation for your unit's future success—and for your own as well."

For Further Reading

Right from the Start: Taking Charge in a New Leadership Role by Dan Ciampa and Michael D. Watkins (1999, Harvard Business School Press)

Taking Charge in Your New Leadership Role: A Workbook by Michael D. Watkins (2001, Harvard Business School Press)

Reprint U0204A

Don't Throw Good Money (or Time) After Bad

❀   ◇   ◎

Jimmy Guterman

You've approved the development of a high-profile new product for your company and now, a year later, things are not going well. Despite forecasts a year ago that customers needed your product, the market has changed and the response is uncertain at best. You're not going to give up and throw away $10 million, are you?

Actually, spending another dime on a doomed product is the wrong decision, say the experts. Chasing after sunk costs, investments that are no longer recoverable, is an error people regularly commit when making decisions.

Just another couple hundred thousand dollars, you say to yourself, *and we'll be able to recoup our prior investment.*

Don't fall for that line of reasoning. True managerial wisdom lies in a kind of forgetfulness—the ability to ignore prior investments, costs, and benefits, and to focus instead on the expected marginal investments, costs, and benefits of the particular decision at hand. But interestingly, people's ability to overlook prior investments seems to vary depending on whether the investment has been one of time or money. Because they're more accustomed to accounting for money, they're more likely to give prior monetary investments undue importance in their deliberations.

When faced with insufficient information and tight time constraints, managers regularly use simplifying strategies, known as *judgment heuristics,* to help them make decision-making shortcuts. Problem is, human psychology always enters into the process, leading to cognitive biases—conclusions based on misperceptions or faulty inferences. The sunk-cost trap is a particular instance of cognitive bias. Max H. Bazerman, Jesse Isidor Straus Professor of Business Administration at Harvard Business School and author of several books, including *Judgment in Managerial Decision Making,* likens this "non-rational escalation of commitment" to standing at a bus stop for hour after hour. At some point, you have to admit that the bus is not coming.

To ensure that you don't escalate your company's commitment to a product, person, or strategy beyond a reasonable point, here are some tried-and-true tips to help you identify the sunk-cost trap before you pour too much money or time down a rat hole.

1: Don't make choices merely to justify past decisions.

Context always influences which decisions get made and how they are made. That said, it's crucial not to let the context obscure the most important goal of decision making: to make sound decisions that are based on the intended future effects, not to legitimate earlier decisions. You don't retain an underperforming, abusive contractor simply because you hired him and you don't want to be accused of flip-flopping. You don't extend additional lines of credit to a struggling company that has consistently failed to meet its obligations just because you made the initial decision to go ahead with the loan and the company promises that just one more loan will turn everything around.

You have to be able to recognize that an earlier decision was a mistake. "A smart manager has to disregard sunk costs and the decisions that led to them," says David E. Bell, a Harvard Business School professor and the author of several books on decision making. "You have to look at the costs and benefits of going forward. Do you keep plowing ahead based on hope or accept the fact that something has not worked?"

One common error that leads to sunk costs: failing to gather external evidence to justify a decision. Here, decision makers pursue sunk costs because they are not considering how people other than their supervisors might view their quandary. When confronted with a choice on whether to move forward on a project, consult as many outside voices and devil's advocates as you can. Overly cautious attitudes toward decision making—which can lead to the sunk-cost trap—are more likely when the decision maker doesn't consider the broader picture or consult outside sources, maintain University of California–Los Angeles professor Shlomo Benartzi and University of Chicago professor Richard H. Thaler in an article for *Management Science*.

As Warren Buffett once said, "When you find yourself in a hole, the best thing you can do is stop digging."

When you look outside, it can be easier to avoid escalation. In 1995, USAir made itself available for sale. Two larger airlines, American and United, were said to be quite interested, and expectations were high that bids would spiral upward—with both American and United committing more and more money, afraid that losing the purchase would make them lose face.

How did American extricate itself from this dubious bidding war? It indicated that it would not bid on USAir—unless United bid first. If that happened, American hinted, expect a bidding war. As it turned out, United didn't make an initial bid, so neither did American. By giving its competition an opportunity to bow out before the offers started, American protected itself from a money-sucking entanglement.

2: Focus on the quality of the decision rather than on the quality of the outcome.

Everybody gets decisions wrong sometimes—even the experts can't forecast every possible outcome. Many decision makers fall for the sunk-cost trap because they fear being judged for the unfortunate consequences of their good-at-the-time decisions. So if you're managing a decision maker, you can prevent unnecessary escalations of commitment by making it clear that no one will be punished for not owning a crystal ball.

"Often people are evaluated, unfortunately, on quality of outcome rather than quality of decision," says Howard Raiffa, a professor emeritus at Harvard Business School. "Very often a change from status quo immediately triggers an evaluation. If decision makers avoid change, the project can limp along without their being held responsible. Good decisions can lead to bad outcomes even for very good decision makers. Any external reviewing process, if there has to be one at that moment, has to take that into account. Otherwise, a person who thinks he'll be fired because of a bad outcome might still pursue the outcome because, hey, it might change and he'll be vindicated. But he knows he'll never be vindicated if he turns back on the original plan."

"Decision makers display a strong bias toward alternatives that perpetuate the status quo," write Raiffa and coauthors John S. Hammond, III, and Ralph L. Keeney in "The Hidden Traps in Decision Making." When things go sour, Raiffa explains, decision makers become "more worried about acts of commission, like changing course, rather than acts of omission, like continuing to take the company down the wrong road. *If I just go along as things are now,* the thinking goes, *things might change. If I commit an act of commission and admit that the current course is wrongheaded, that may trigger a review process at an unwanted time.* There are huge internal and external pressures to keep going even if all parties realize it's wrong and it's going to stay wrong."

"Sunk-time costs come when people are in a rut and afraid to think," says Raiffa. "People think their project is going poorly, their life is going poorly, but they're stuck and afraid to change. They're so emotionally involved they just stick with the status quo. The enlightened manager needs to see this happening, in himself and others, and pull himself out of the trap."

3: The more you equate time with money, the more susceptible you are to the sunk-cost trap.

That's the conclusion Hong Kong University of Science and Technology marketing professor Dilip Soman reaches based on a series of sunk-cost experiments he conducted. As he notes in a recent article in the *Journal of Behavioral Decision Making,* the sunk-cost trap tends not to appear when the investment has been one of time. But as people become more adept in their mental accounting for time—that is, as they're able to convert an investment of time into a monetary equivalent—their decisions are more likely to be skewed by sunk-time costs.

4: Use decision rules to prevent cloudy thinking.

In *Judgment in Managerial Decision Making,* Bazerman identifies a common scenario: "You personally decided to hire a new middle-level manager to work for you. Although you had expected excellent performance, early reports suggest that she is not performing as you had hoped. Should you fire her? Perhaps you really can't afford her current level of performance. On the other hand, you have invested a fair amount in her training. Furthermore, she may just be in the process of learning the ropes. So you decide to invest in her a bit longer and provide additional resources so that she can succeed. But still she does not perform as expected. Although you have more reason to 'cut your losses,' you now have even more invested in this employee."

> Many decision makers fall for the sunk-cost trap because they fear being judged for the unfortunate consequences of their good-at-the-time decisions.

Precise targets can help you avoid this endless round of rationalizing earlier decisions. If you've established in advance how much time and money you're willing to invest in a project or person before you begin to see specific results, you're less likely fall into the sunk-cost trap. As the investment sage Warren Buffett once said, "When you find yourself in a hole, the best thing you can do is stop digging." Such targets tell you when to put down the shovel. They enable you to discriminate, says Bazerman, "between situations in which persistence will pay off and situations in which it will not."

For Further Reading

Judgment in Managerial Decision Making, 5e by Max H. Bazerman (2001, John Wiley & Sons)

"The Mental Accounting of Sunk Time Costs" by Dilip Soman (*Journal of Behavioral Decision Making,* Vol. 14, 2001)

"Risk Aversion or Myopia?" by Shlomo Benartzi and Richard H. Thaler (*Management Science,* Vol. 45, No. 3, March 1999)

"The Hidden Traps in Decision Making" by John S. Hammond, III, Ralph L. Keeney, and Howard Raiffa (*Harvard Business Review,* September–October 1998)

Reprint U0205D

Which Projects Get Top Billing?

o   o   o

Paul Michelman

You can't do it all, so what will you do? What's best for your career, what's best for your team, or what's best for the firm? Grab the low-hanging fruit, or reach for the stars?

Choosing which projects to pursue and which to let languish is among the most difficult and important decisions any executive faces. "There are always more productive tasks for tomorrow than there is time to do them and more opportunities than there are capable people to take care of them," notes Peter Drucker in his classic *The Effective Executive* (HarperCollins, 1967). Thus the need for prioritizing is continual. "The only question is which will make the decision," Drucker writes, "the executive or the pressures." If the pressures "are allowed to make the decision, the important tasks will predictably be sacrificed."

In other words, if you want to have the greatest possible impact, you need to remain in control of your own priority setting. Start by asking a few simple questions. B.J. Gallagher, former training manager for the *Los Angeles Times* and coauthor of *A Peacock in the Land of Penguins: A Fable About Creativity and Courage* (3rd ed., Berrett-Koehler, 2001), suggests these:

- Which "to do" will have the biggest impact on my team and my organization?

- Which is important to my boss?

- Which might make a big difference in my personal success?

- Which will have the biggest negative impact if I don't do it?

Ideally, you'll want to tackle a mix of projects that, in total, will benefit your company, your boss, your team, *and* yourself. Put at the top those projects that benefit the broadest cross-section of these constituencies.

Projects should also be analyzed "by how they relate to one's 'focused intent,'" says Howard Goldman, author of *Choose What Works* (Wynnefield Business Press, 2004). "Focused intent is the intersection of long-term strategy and critical deliverables that validate the long term."

In setting your priorities, look first at how each of your potential projects aligns with corporate strategy, and consider which can most effectively move the company toward its goals. If returning to growth is a priority, focus on what you can do to help boost the top line. How can you have the biggest impact on gaining new customers, increasing sales, or expanding distribution?

And then get even more specific. If you are a manager charged with increasing sales, says Annette Richmond, principal of Richmond Consulting Group, consider these questions: "What will help you the most? New marketing materials? Additional staff? Change of strategy? Choose the project that will have the most immediate impact."

Next, look at which of your projects most directly supports your boss's goals for the coming year. When in doubt, ask.

Then look at your team's needs. How can you best support your team members in reaching departmental goals? Be careful not to dismiss seemingly smaller projects that will help your direct reports reach performance objectives. Your support here can pay big dividends in terms of loyalty.

Once you've considered the strategic goals of the company, the priorities of your boss, and the needs of your team, look at how these stack up against your personal targets. On one hand, placing the "greater good" above your own personal pursuits can position you as a team player with a broad strategic vision. On the other hand, not all organizations are adept at spotting people who act quite so selflessly. So you can't make these choices in a vacuum.

"Setting priorities is a collaborative effort," says management consultant Kristin Arnold. Sit down with your boss and "discuss the strategic and business plans, the current projects and potential projects over the next year. Once you have the list of possibilities, then jointly prioritize the list," she says.

Setting your priorities is only half the battle; some would say it's the easy half. You must then display the courage of your convictions, particularly when it comes to the *posteriorities*—the projects that don't get top billing. "Every posteriority is somebody else's top priority," writes Drucker. "It is much easier to draw up a nice list of top priorities and then to hedge by trying to do 'just a little bit' of everything else as well. This makes everybody happy. The only drawback is that nothing whatsoever gets done."

Reprint U0404D

Preventing Burnout

o   o   o

Time-starved managers are notoriously at risk for burnout—a condition that's damaging for you *and* your company. But there's good news: Experts have identified plenty of disciplines, routines, and easy practices you can incorporate into your life to keep burnout at bay.

As you'll find in this section's articles, even small changes—such as having a suitcase packed ahead of time for business travel—can hugely ease the stress associated with time pressure. Relaxation disciplines (such as meditation or yoga) and plain old healthy living (including eating right and exercising regularly) also go a long way toward preventing burnout. And don't forget the value of delegating: By refusing to take on tasks that should be handled by your direct reports, you reduce your own stress, refocus on your higher priorities, and encourage your team members to develop their professional skills. Together, all these practices help you reduce the risk of burnout. You, your employees, and your firm all benefit.

Making Sense of Your Time Bind, and Escaping It

○   ○   ○

David Stauffer

Do you recognize yourself in these descriptions?

"Gwen's workday . . . is regularly eight and a half to nine hours, not counting the work that often spills over into life at home.

"Gwen's stories are . . . about coming home to a refrigerator containing little more than wilted lettuce and a jar of olives, stories told in a spirit of hopeless amusement.

"There were, in a sense, two Bell households: the rushed family they actually were and the relaxed family they imagined they could be if only they had the time."

Arlie Russell Hochschild, a sociology professor at the University of California, Berkeley, describes the Bell's situation (pseudonyms are used) in *The Time Bind*. The work summarizes the research of three summers Hochschild spent "following around" more than 100 headquarters employees of an unidentified *Fortune* 500 company. If the situations she describes ring a familiar chord, you are among the vast number of Americans—hard-working, conscientious, and law-abiding (other than driving everywhere too fast)—who feel incredibly pressed for time.

> Move away from the idea that certain activities must continually give way to the "demands" of other activities.

Hochschild leaves little doubt that the time-starved deserve better. However, she also apparently believes there is little that individuals can do on their own to make things better: "Parents now increasingly . . . speak of time as if it were a threatened form of personal capital . . . whose value seems to rise and fall according to forces beyond their control."

The sociologist lists and rejects a number of ways "to deal with the time bind as a purely personal problem, and to develop personal strategies for coping with it in one's own life." She vigorously advocates the idea that "unknotting the time bind requires collective—rather than individual—action: Workers must directly challenge the organization, and the organizers, of the American workplace."

Hochschild's nearly total reliance on collective action comes as a bit of a surprise, in light of the many techniques for easing the time crunch advocated by smart people across the U.S. They report that there are in fact ways for individuals and families to wrestle, and sometimes tame, the scheduling beast, contrary to the central conclusion in *The Time Bind*.

1: Reverse Your Relationship to Time

The only way to free yourself from the grip of time, and to get a grip on it, is to first make a fundamental shift in how you think about it. Move away from the idea that certain activities must continually give way to the "demands" of other activities. Move toward the idea that activities you value are as important as what you feel compelled to do; indeed, that they are inviolable. Here are some ways you might do that.

Keep Your Focus on What's Really Important

"It's much easier to be very busy than to be very effective," says A. Roger Merrill, of the Franklin Covey Company. Merrill does not dispute the increasing pressure you may feel from too much to do in too little time. "But we too easily blur what should be a critical distinction between what's urgent and what's important. Urgency can become an addiction."

So put important things first. The wisdom of doing so becomes clear during a real crisis, says Stanford School of Medicine stress management researcher Dr. Kenneth R. Pelletier. "When a child is ill or a parent dies, we have immediate reminders of what's important and our priorities become very clear."

Change Your Self-Talk

Consider employing what organizational psychologist Donald Moine calls affirmations. "When you're engaged in a task, you're always talking to yourself about it," he observes, adding that such messages are extremely powerful. "You can make the outcome you expect actually happen," he argues. Try repeating positive affirmations—for example, "I'm in control of how I spend my time"—over and over again. The exercise is "essential" to achieve the desired result.

Acknowledge That You Can't Do It All

In his book *Information Anxiety,* iconoclast Richard Saul Wurman says many of us help create the time pressures we perceive by, for example, subscribing to a host of newspapers and magazines: "You greet each one as if it will [confirm] your membership in the elite Informed Persons Club." But there will always be more publications, and more potential demands on your time, than you can possibly keep up with. Wurman argues that the solution lies in recognizing that you can't do everything and "narrowing your field" by making tough choices about what merits your attention.

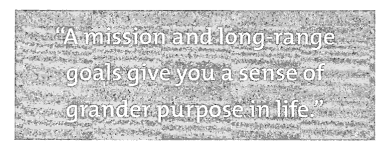

"A mission and long-range goals give you a sense of grander purpose in life."

Enjoy the Doing, Not Just Getting Done

"Hurry sickness" is a concept developed by psychologist Bruce A. Baldwin, who heads the consulting firm Direction Dynamics. He attributes hurry sickness to "the progressive need for task completion." As part of his prescription for curing this illness, Baldwin says you should come to terms with the "inevitable problems and delays that are part of life" and enjoy your experiences so you "will find yourself wanting to prolong [an activity] because you are having such a good time!"

2: Decide Where You Want to Go and Plan to Get There

It's an old, familiar lesson, but bears repeating if only for the legions who keep forgetting: Time should be treated as a resource, says Jack D. Ferner, a professor of management at Wake Forest University, "allocated where it is most needed." But when it comes to this particular resource, he notes, allocations to the most important things "seem to be deferred over and over again." He reiterates the enduring verity—that goal setting is the first step to more appropriate time allocation. The experts have many suggestions for how to go about this.

Set Long-Term Objectives

Stanford's Pelletier says a famous polar explorer once told him, "You can go faster and faster around the equator, but you'll never get to the North Pole."

So bite the bullet and figure out what you want to have accomplished at the end of the long haul. Andrew J. DuBrin, a consultant and management professor at the Rochester Institute of Technology, offers the most important reasons for doing this: "A mission and long-range goals give you a sense of grander purpose in life.

You better position yourself in relation to work, family, and community. I believe you're also better able to put up with the little frustrations anyone encounters."

Don't take this to mean that these goals must guide your every action. That would just replace one kind of time prison with another. But if you get the goals on paper, and put them where you'll see them once or twice a month, you may be surprised to find how they help save time—perhaps because they serve implicitly as priority-setters.

Make a Standing Weekly Schedule

Look at the way you want to spend your time in terms of categories of activities—job, chores, exercise, activities with family, unstructured relaxation, and so forth. Figure the number of hours weekly you're going to spend in each category.

Once you've drawn up your general weekly schedule, use it to help you keep track, as each week passes, of approximately where you stand in relation to the time allotted for each major category. As you approach the end of the week, try to give more time to the activities that got short shrift at the beginning of the week.

Set Key Weekly and Daily Objectives

Once you have your standing weekly schedule, you're ready to customize it by planning each week at the start of those seven days. Stephen Covey and his associates advise a weekly family gathering around the dining room table, at which each person talks about his or her obligations and chief objectives for the coming week. Family members help keep you from allowing those urgent but unimportant things to crowd out the important things related to your long-term goals.

Similarly, but on an individual and less formal basis, start each day by making a list of the top three or four things you want to accomplish that day. Stanford's Pelletier describes this as "a deceptively simple exercise that has been shown to significantly help people focus and not so often get to the end of a day feeling frustrated."

3: Spend More Time on Neglected Essentials

To escape the time bind, use some of your time for activities that allow you to be more productive all of the time.

Exercise As If Your Life Depends on It

(It does.) Accumulating research data indicate that the time spent on regular physical exercise is more than paid back in greater overall personal productivity. One study, for example, showed that workers who exercise regularly are absent about half as many days and file about half the health insurance claims, measured in dollar value, as employees who don't exercise.

Stop Running a Sleep Deficit

"In the early 1900s people were sleeping an average of 8 1/2 hours each night," says Timothy Roehrs, professor of psychiatry at Wayne State University and research director of the Henry Ford Hospital Sleep Disorders and Research Center in Detroit. "The average now is 7 1/2 hours." Roehrs says the majority of us need that "lost" hour, which "results for most people in about a 20% loss of performance efficiency."

Don't Neglect the Spiritual

In *The 7 Habits of Highly Effective People,* Stephen Covey cites the quote attributed to Martin Luther—"I have so much to do today, I'll need to spend another hour on my knees"—to convey the idea that "when we take time to draw on the [spiritual dimension], . . . it spreads like an umbrella over everything else." Covey associate Roger Merrill argues that regular reading of classic works of inspiration can aid the effort to get more done. "Participants in my seminars uniformly report an amazing effect of devoting just 10 or 15 minutes each day to such works."

Take Time to Do Nothing

Psychologist Bruce A. Baldwin lists "irrational beliefs" about relaxation and "corrections" that state the rational facts of the matter, including

- LEISURE TIME IS JUSTIFIED ONLY AS A REWARD FOR HARD WORK.
  Correction: Regard leisure time as a "health mandate."

- THERE CAN BE NO RELAXATION WHILE THERE'S WORK TO BE DONE.
  Correction: The work is never done, so "you must accept your work as an ongoing process."

- IF YOU LET YOURSELF RELAX, YOUR INHERENT LAZINESS WILL BURST THROUGH.
  Correction: You're not lazy, you're tired! You must relax and emotionally recharge just like other people.

4: Choose Time Management Techniques That Are Right for You

Hochschild questions the ultimate value of long-standing time-management techniques: "Paradoxically, what may seem to harried working parents like a solution to their time bind—efficiency and time segmentation—can later feel like a problem in itself." But there are creative ways to resist becoming overwhelmed by time management as well as everything else.

Just Say "No"

"By saying 'yes' when we really want to say 'no,' we're taking a short-term gain at the cost of long-term pain," says consultant Barbara J. Braham. She argues that we can, and must, reverse the gain-pain effect by saying no when we don't want to do something. Among the benefits that she counts: "We reduce stress, boost productivity, and gain control of our lives—by exercising our ability to make choices."

Resist the Urge to Make Everything Perfect

Miriam Adderholdt-Elliott, a former professor of education at the University of North Carolina at Charlotte, describes herself as a "recovering" perfectionist. The perfectionist can't let go of a project, she observes, because it's never exactly right. Learn when to quit. Recognize a point of diminishing returns and move on to something else.

Yes, Organize, but Do So in a Way That Suits You

"The popular methods of time management—making to-do lists, keeping your desk clear, filing systematically—were designed by and for linear thinkers," says consultant and admitted non-linear thinker Ann McGee-Cooper. On the other shore, she says, are divergent thinkers, who are more comfortable with a stacked desk top, seat-of-the-pants schedules, and juggling several tasks at once. For those people, McGee-Cooper recommends a desk top with ordered stacks of papers, perhaps placed in colored file folders or wire baskets. "Your linear-thinking visitors, perhaps including your boss, will then see 'visual order' rather than 'out of control.'"

For Further Reading

First Things First: To Live, To Love, To Learn, To Leave a Legacy by A. Roger Merrill, Stephen R. Covey, and Rebecca R. Merrill (1994, Simon & Schuster)

Getting It Done: The Transforming Power of Self-Discipline by Andrew J. DuBrin (1995, Peterson's/Pacesetter Books)

It's All in Your Head: Lifestyle Management Strategies for Busy People by Bruce A. Baldwin (1985, Direction Dynamics)

The Perfectionist Predicament by Miriam Adderholdt-Elliott and Susan Meltsner (1991, Morrow)

Sound Mind, Sound Body by Kenneth R. Pelletier (1994, Simon & Schuster)

Successful Time Management: A Self-Teaching Guide by Jack D. Ferner (1995, John Wiley & Sons)

The Time Bind by Arlie Russell Hochschild (1997, Metropolitan/Henry Holt)

Time Management for Unmanageable People by Ann McGee-Cooper (1994, Bantam)

Reprint U9708B

Pump Up Your Volume!

A Dozen Ideas for Boosting Personal Productivity

o   ©   ©

David Stauffer

Americans seek to put extra pep in their day with momentarily popular potions from Geritol to ginseng. Not being of a pharmaceutical orientation, *Harvard Management Update* took the approach it knows best and consulted the experts.

Like you, these folks—accomplished in a variety of fields related to personal productivity—face more demand than ever on their time and energy. We asked for solutions that work for them and might do the trick for you, too. So read on, take note, and give yourself a kick in your capacity.

1: Accept Our Imperfect World

Abandon perfectionism, urges consultant and motivational speaker Wolf J. Rinke, who heads his own firm in Clarksville, Maryland. "Managers who are afflicted with perfectionism accomplish relatively little," Rinke claims, "because they are unable to delegate and give their power away." The problem: "Life, people, business, and even nature are imperfect." The solution: "Accept imperfection as the normal order of things. But expect the best, because most of the time you'll get what you expect."

2: Add Ounces of Prevention

As president of the American Institute for Preventive Medicine in Farmington Hills, Michigan, Don R. Powell says, "I try to practice what I preach to increase my personal productivity." That entails good-health habits that many of us know well and practice sporadically: "I eat breakfast every day, try not to snack, limit fats and cholesterol, and maintain a good body weight-to-height ratio. To exercise regularly, I play tennis and jog. For stress management, I meditate twice daily." Acknowledging that "it's not easy to change lifestyles," Powell says the key is "to make small changes over time rather than trying to alter your behavior all at once."

3: Shape Up That Cerebral Cortex

Think your productivity would soar if only your memory was better? Join the crowd. "These days, more people are complaining about memory inadequacies because we have so much more to remember," says Barry Gordon, M.D., professor of neurology and director of the Johns Hopkins Memory Clinic in Baltimore, Maryland. "Remember when your total television fare consisted of four channels and no remote control?"

Be selective in choosing what to remember, Gordon advises, "because you can't remember it all. And always carry a pencil and paper." Whenever possible, repeat what you choose to remember. "Any active involvement, such as repetition, gives memory a jolt that's missing when you passively receive information." Involve the senses, for example, remembering not just "apple," but also "red," "juicy," "pie," and "Mom." These "multiple encodings" are stored in different brain locations. "The more encodings we have, the more likely we are to remember," says Gordon.

If you're sharp enough to be worried about your memory, Gordon adds, "your memory is almost certainly just fine." Age has only two pervasive effects on memory: you've got lots more knowledge to sort through for retrieval, and processing time slows as you get older. "But studies show that, given a little more time, older folks' memories are as good as youngsters'," Gordon observes.

4: Flush Away Bad Stress

"Some stress is good; it makes us get up and do something," says Bruce Munro, director of behavioral medicine for the Jackson Hole Institute of Stress Medicine in Wilson, Wyoming. Bad stress arises from things we feel we can't control. "The trick is to find a way to feel that we have some measure of control, even if it's not currently possible to actually have control."

Sometimes, Munro says, that means fabricating control. "I'll tell a patient to walk in the bathroom and flush the toilet. That—or a similar seemingly pointless action—can break the constant cycling of stress, where the effects of one immediate stressor spill over to other areas." Such tactics help get stress to "a usable level, where we gain a sense of control and turn it from bad to good."

5: Beat the (Circadian) Clock

Stanford University neuroscience professor Robert Sapolsky says he's coping with a new source of joy—and stress—his first child. "I've had to become vastly more efficient about time." His key target: "Combating the mid-afternoon slows. I now do all my exercising at mid-day, just before a very light lunch, to remain alert in the afternoon. I do all my reading in the first few hours of the day, then my sustained writing, and then work such as returning phone calls and writing e-mail messages." Sapolsky recommends "circadian" awareness, "matching your best and worst times of the day to your most demanding and most mindless work."

Consultant Andrew J. DuBrin came to the circadian solution by a different path. "Earlier this year I traced a drop in my productivity to spending too much of my prime time on e-mail—including getting my e-mail system fixed," says the Rochester Institute of Technology management professor. "Except in emergencies, I now almost never deal with e-mail or the Internet during prime time."

6: Catch Callers in Your Web

Professional organizer Lisa Kanarek, who heads Dallas-based Everything's Organized, offers this productivity tip: "I've added my Web address to my voice mail message. Many callers simply download my information, saving time for them and me."

7: Take the Long View and Back Up

Executive coach and leadership consultant James B. Anderson, president of Anderson Leadership Group in

Vienna, Virginia, recommends two "interrelated" productivity boosters.

Vision Check-Ups

"I'm not talking eyesight, but looking far ahead, to where you want to be 10 years from now. Then you back up to the present: five years out, next year, next month, and next week. This tells you if you're moving at this moment toward where you want to be in 10 years."

R, R & R Getaways

That's rest, relax, and rethink. "You're not just recharging your batteries," Anderson remarks, "you're also taking a step back, looking at where you've been and where you want to go."

8: Connect to Control Worry

According to Harvard Medical School lecturer Edward M. Hallowell, M.D., "toxic" unproductive worry "eats at the heart of many people in business today." His prescription for neutralizing its effects is "connectedness . . . a feeling of being part of something larger than yourself."

Hallowell's steps toward connectedness in the workplace include: "Saying hello. Setting up lunch dates. Sending friendly or whimsical e-mail. . . . Humor, spontaneity, laughter. . . . Take an interest in other people's work. Ask for advice. The connected workplace is one that values the opinions of others. Without connectedness, you worry. With it, you thrive."

9: Learn How to Succeed on $2

"In 97 of 100 cases, we know how to make a change we desire," says Jonathan Robinson, a psychotherapist and seminar leader in Santa Barbara, California. "The barrier isn't lack of wisdom, it's lack of motivation." Robinson's solution? "Make a contract with yourself that lists specific accomplishments for the coming week. For every one you haven't reached by the deadline, you rip up $2. . . . For almost everyone, the pain of literally ripping up money is greater than the pain of skipping a snack or exercising or performing some other targeted action."

10: Get Carried Away with Flow

"Flow is the unique feeling you have when you're totally engaged in your work," says University of Chicago psychology professor Mihaly Csikszentmihalyi. "When you're in flow, your activity seems to carry you along effortlessly, as though by the strong current of a stream. . . . The activity is its own reward. Hours pass like minutes, and you lose awareness of what's going on around you."

To experience flow more often, Csikszentmihalyi advises, "try to spend more time on the things you enjoy doing most. Also, expand your range of activities. And don't only look outside your job; people more often find flow in their work than in non-work activities."

11: Tally Each Day's *Bests* and *Could-Be-Betters*

Executive coach Richard D. Buckingham, who heads Goal-Star Business Strategies in Bethesda, Maryland, suggests concluding your day (or week or project) with the "Liked Best, Next Time" exercise. Write down the two or three things you did that were most personally pleasing to you—for example, accomplishing a goal or performing better. Then, list the things you'd like to improve in some way the next time.

"The Liked Best list is an important pat on the back," Buckingham explains. "The Next Time list provides specific targets to keep doing better."

12: Jump for Joy

"Without regularly refreshing yourself with fun and child-like play," says Dallas consultant Ann McGee-Cooper, "you will get less and less done in more and more time." She recounts the story of a client group that had been putting in seven-day weeks. When "faced with a huge new challenge," their response was to spend a day on a farm, "shooting tin cans off fence posts, swinging on vines, and playing basketball." Later, like magic, "they came up with fantastic solutions" to their new work problems. "It wouldn't have happened without getting out of their rut and having fun."

For Further Reading

Finding Flow: The Psychology of Engagement with Everyday Life by Mihaly Csikszentmihaly (1998, reprint edition, Basic Books)

Getting It Done: The Transforming Power of Self-Discipline by Andrew J. DuBrin (1995, Peterson's/Pacesetter Books)

Memory: Remembering and Forgetting in Everyday Life by Barry Gordon (1996, Intelligence Amplification)

Organize Your Home Office for Success by Lisa Kanarek (1998, Blakely Press)

Time Management for Unmanageable People by Ann McGee-Cooper (1994, Bantam)

Worry: Controlling It and Using It Wisely by Edward M. Hallowell (1997, Pantheon)

Reprint U9809D

Five Questions About Encouraging Managers to Delegate with Jeffrey Pfeffer

○　　○　　○

Managers' common reluctance to delegate responsibility is a topic that has long intrigued Jeffrey Pfeffer, coauthor, with Charles O'Reilly, of *Hidden Value: How Great Companies Achieve Extraordinary Results with Ordinary People*

(Harvard Business School Press, 2000). Pfeffer says that there is mounting evidence that giving people more responsibility for making decisions in their jobs generates greater productivity, morale, and commitment. Yet despite these benefits, many managers are reluctant to cede control. *Harvard Management Update* recently asked Pfeffer, whose research helps explain the reasons for such reluctance, what companies can do to overcome it.

1. What is the most effective step companies can take to encourage managers to delegate more responsibility?

One of the primary ways we learn is by observing what people around us do. So, if I want you to delegate more and micromanage less, then I need to reflect that in my own behavior. The first place every manager looks to determine the most appropriate way to act is at their superiors.

2. How do you persuasively describe the value of delegating to a subordinate?

I don't think one "describes" the value of delegation, at least as a way of changing behavior. The best thing to do is some form of experiential exercise in which people are "shown" the benefits of delegation and the costs of not doing so. Some of those exercises involve problem-solving exercises in which people learn that not accessing the expertise of others leads to worse solutions.

Some of the exercises involve having people be supervised. The most powerful is called "star power" and has people experience what it is to be powerless—something that provokes strong reactions, to put it mildly. Believe me, "telling" people the benefits of delegation has no effect at all, as the failure to follow the advice of the numerous books and articles that do just that attest.

3. Is organizational structure a factor?

Absolutely. It affects behavior in two ways. First, it sends signals to managers about the type of behavior the organization finds most acceptable. For example, in a relatively flat organizational structure where there are few management layers and managers have broad spans of control, people understand that delegation is the norm. Second, in a very real sense, structure either facilitates or hinders delegation by the nature and strength of the boundaries it erects.

 One way companies can compel increased delegation is to assign managers larger staffs and more responsibility. The larger a manager's staff becomes, the less he/she will be able to micromanage them.

4. Is there too much focus being placed on leadership?

Yes, and the problem extends beyond companies to include the business press, but that's another story. If your organization venerates heroic leaders, then your managers are going to have a natural reluctance to delegate responsibility.

One of the ways companies encourage heroic leaders is by providing them with a host of highly visible trappings, from elegant offices and reserved parking to executive dining rooms and travel on private jets. It's frequently difficult for managers with such perks to entrust responsibility to subordinates whose trappings are significantly inferior to their own.

Organizations in which the spirit of delegating prevails tend to be those with an egalitarian culture that is manifested in such things as open office arrangements and the lack of status symbols. These help build the sense among workers that they are relatively equal.

5. Can recruiting be employed to encourage delegation?

This is another important step that companies can take. Hiring people who are by nature autocratic will certainly mitigate against building an organization that values teamwork.

How do you determine a candidate's management style? Unquestionably, the most reliable predictor is past behavior. Management style reflects a certain mindset and therefore is difficult to change. So companies should look carefully at the ways candidates have approached their responsibilities at their prior employers.

Related to past performance is the nature of the management environment in the organizations where the candidate has worked. If they fared well in an organization that's known to be team-driven, then they'll likely be comfortable with delegating responsibilities in their new role.

Reprint U0401D

About the Contributors

Melissa Raffoni is a consultant who specializes in organizational development and executive coaching. She is also a lecturer at the MIT Sloan School of Business.

Paul Michelman is editor of *Harvard Management Update*.

Jim Billington is a contributor to *Harvard Management Update*.

Constantine von Hoffman is a contributor to *Harvard Management Update*.

Tom Krattenmaker is a freelance writer and director of news and information at Swarthmore College, near Philadelphia.

Dwight Moore is an industrial psychologist with the firm Moore & Associates in Blaine, Washington.

Edward Prewitt is a contributor to *Harvard Management Update*.

Jennifer McFarland is a freelance writer based in Somerville, Massachusetts.

Robert J. Thomas is a senior research fellow at Accenture's Institute for Strategic Change in Cambridge, Massachusetts. **Warren Bennis** is University Professor and founding chairman of the Leadership Institute at the University of Southern California. They are coauthors of *Geeks and Geezers: How Era, Values, and Defining Moments Shape Leaders* (Harvard Business School Press, 2002).

About the Contributors

Jimmy Guterman is president of the Vineyard Group, Inc., a consultancy in Chestnut Hill, Massachusetts. He is also the publisher of *Media Unspun*.

David Stauffer is a contributor to *Harvard Management Update*.

Harvard Business Review Paperback Series

The Harvard Business Review Paperback Series offers the best thinking on cutting-edge management ideas from the world's leading thinkers, researchers, and managers. Designed for leaders who believe in the power of ideas to change business, these books will be useful to managers at all levels of experience, but especially senior executives and general managers. In addition, this series is widely used in training and executive development programs.

Books are priced at $19.95 U.S.
Price subject to change.

Title	Product #
Harvard Business Review **Interviews with CEOs**	3294
Harvard Business Review on **Advances in Strategy**	8032
Harvard Business Review on **Becoming a High Performance Manager**	1296
Harvard Business Review on **Brand Management**	1445
Harvard Business Review on **Breakthrough Leadership**	8059
Harvard Business Review on **Breakthrough Thinking**	181X
Harvard Business Review on **Building Personal and Organizational Resilience**	2721
Harvard Business Review on **Business and the Environment**	2336
Harvard Business Review on **Change**	8842
Harvard Business Review on **Compensation**	701X
Harvard Business Review on **Corporate Ethics**	273X
Harvard Business Review on **Corporate Governance**	2379
Harvard Business Review on **Corporate Responsibility**	2748
Harvard Business Review on **Corporate Strategy**	1429
Harvard Business Review on **Crisis Management**	2352
Harvard Business Review on **Culture and Change**	8369
Harvard Business Review on **Customer Relationship Management**	6994
Harvard Business Review on **Decision Making**	5572
Harvard Business Review on **Effective Communication**	1437

To order, call 1-800-668-6780, or go online at www.HBSPress.org

Title	Product #
Harvard Business Review on **Entrepreneurship**	9105
Harvard Business Review on **Finding and Keeping the Best People**	5564
Harvard Business Review on **Innovation**	6145
Harvard Business Review on **Knowledge Management**	8818
Harvard Business Review on **Leadership**	8834
Harvard Business Review on **Leadership at the Top**	2756
Harvard Business Review on **Leading in Turbulent Times**	1806
Harvard Business Review on **Managing Diversity**	7001
Harvard Business Review on **Managing High-Tech Industries**	1828
Harvard Business Review on **Managing People**	9075
Harvard Business Review on **Managing the Value Chain**	2344
Harvard Business Review on **Managing Uncertainty**	9083
Harvard Business Review on **Managing Your Career**	1318
Harvard Business Review on **Marketing**	8040
Harvard Business Review on **Measuring Corporate Performance**	8826
Harvard Business Review on **Mergers and Acquisitions**	5556
Harvard Business Review on **Motivating People**	1326
Harvard Business Review on **Negotiation**	2360
Harvard Business Review on **Nonprofits**	9091
Harvard Business Review on **Organizational Learning**	6153
Harvard Business Review on **Strategic Alliances**	1334
Harvard Business Review on **Strategies for Growth**	8850
Harvard Business Review on **The Business Value of IT**	9121
Harvard Business Review on **The Innovative Enterprise**	130X
Harvard Business Review on **Turnarounds**	6366
Harvard Business Review on **What Makes a Leader**	6374
Harvard Business Review on **Work and Life Balance**	3286

Management Dilemmas: Case Studies from the Pages of Harvard Business Review

How often do you wish you could turn to a panel of experts to guide you through tough management situations? The Management Dilemmas series provides just that. Drawn from the pages of *Harvard Business Review,* each insightful volume poses several perplexing predicaments and shares the problem-solving wisdom of leading experts. Engagingly written, these solutions-oriented collections help managers make sound judgment calls when addressing everyday management dilemmas.

These books are priced at $19.95 U.S.
Price subject to change.

Title	Product #
Management Dilemmas: **When Change Comes Undone**	5038
Management Dilemmas: **When Good People Behave Badly**	5046
Management Dilemmas: **When Marketing Becomes a Minefield**	290X

Harvard Business Essentials

In the fast-paced world of business today, everyone needs a personal resource—a place to go for advice, coaching, background information, or answers. The Harvard Business Essentials series fits the bill. Concise and straightforward, these books provide highly practical advice for readers at all levels of experience. Whether you are a new manager interested in expanding your skills or an experienced executive looking to stay on top, these solution-oriented books give you the reliable tips and tools you need to improve your performance and get the job done. Harvard Business Essentials titles will quickly become your constant companions and trusted guides.

These books are priced at $19.95 U.S., except as noted.
Price subject to change.

Title	Product #
Harvard Business Essentials: **Negotiation**	1113
Harvard Business Essentials: **Managing Creativity and Innovation**	1121
Harvard Business Essentials: **Managing Change and Transition**	8741
Harvard Business Essentials: **Hiring and Keeping the Best People**	875X
Harvard Business Essentials: **Finance for Managers**	8768
Harvard Business Essentials: **Business Communication**	113X
Harvard Business Essentials: **Manager's Toolkit ($24.95)**	2896
Harvard Business Essentials: **Managing Projects Large and Small**	3213
Harvard Business Essentials: **Creating Teams with an Edge**	290X

The Results-Driven Manager

The Results-Driven Manager series collects timely articles from *Harvard Management Update* and *Harvard Management Communication Letter* to help senior to middle managers sharpen their skills, increase their effectiveness, and gain a competitive edge. Presented in a concise, accessible format to save managers valuable time, these books offer authoritative insights and techniques for improving job performance and achieving immediate results.

These books are priced at $14.95 U.S.
Price subject to change.

Readers of the Results-Driven Manager series find the following Harvard Business School Press books of interest.

If you find these books useful:	You may also like these:
Presentations That Persuade and Motivate Getting People on Board	Working the Room (8199)
Face-to-Face Communications for Clarity and Impact Dealing with Difficult People	HBR on Effective Communication (1437) HBR on Managing People (9075)
Winning Negotiations That Preserve Relationships	HBR on Negotiation (2360) HBE Guide to Negotiation (1113)
Teams That Click	The Wisdom of Teams (3670) Leading Teams (3332)
Managing Yourself for the Career You Want Taking Control of Your Time	Primal Leadership (486X) Leading Quietly (4878) Leadership on the Line (4371)

To order, call 1-800-668-6780, or go online at www.HBSPress.org

How to Order

Harvard Business School Press publications are available worldwide
from your local bookseller or online retailer.
You can also call

1-800-668-6780

Our product consultants are available to help you
8:00 a.m.–6:00 p.m., Monday–Friday, Eastern Time.
Outside the U.S. and Canada, call: 617-783-7450
Please call about special discounts for quantities greater than ten.

You can order online at

www.HBSPress.org